D0735135

LAST WALK
ON
OUR BLOCK

A Family's Journey Through Time

By

Ron Baumbach

Williston Park Public Library

8/9/12

Ron Board

Thanks for
the walk!

All rights reserved. No part of this publication may be reproduced or transmitted in any form or by any means electronic or mechanical, including photography, recording, or any information storage and retrieval system now known or to be invented, without permission in writing from the author.

While the occurrences in this book did indeed happen, some of the people have been fictionalized and any resemblance to people living or dead is purely coincidental. If in reading this you believe you recognize yourself and it makes you feel good, that's nice. If it does the opposite, then it certainly cannot be you.

Cover photo by Kaitlin M. Baumbach

With grateful appreciation to Paul Cassone for permission to reprint "Here's To Good Friends"
http://www.myspace.com/paulcassone

House photos via public domain records:
http://www.nassaucountyny.gov/mynassauproperty/main.jsp

The Last Walk on Our Block Copyright © 2011 by Ron Baumbach
ISBN-13: 978-1466473621
ISBN-10: 1466473622
LCCN - Library of Congress Control Number: 2011962589

2012
A www.competell.com creation

Made in the USA
Lexington, KY
22 March 2012

14341156R00198

GAYLORD

WILLISTON PARK PUBLIC LIBRARY
494 WILLIS AVENUE
WILLISTON PARK, NY 11596
516-742-1820
www.willistonparklibrary.org

11/2/-17
7/20-17
9/9/16 - 16
9/25/13 - 8.

WITHDRAWN

3/29/2012   12.95

B
Baumbach, Ron
The Last Walk on Our Block:
A Family Journey Through Time

BIOGRAPHY

Williston Park Public Library

Williston Park Public Library

About the Author:

Ron Baumbach is an American who has been most enriched in his life.

He proudly carries his wealth in his wallet in the form of his most cherished family photos.

The Four Block Walkers
e 1958
Deb, Ron, Jerry, Dick

Dedication

From an obvious standpoint, a book about one's upbringing would be justified to be dedicated to those who both brought you into the world and then up in the world. How can I be any different?

For Mom and Dad, I thank you for providing me life, love, guidance and a bonded family to share the beginnings of a wonderful journey. I am forever grateful, and while you are not now with us in body, your spirit has truly aided in this reflection.

For my siblings Dick, Jerry and Deb, I thank you for taking the walk with me and for being a most significant part of the treasure that we created and molded together. For their spouses Diane and Elaine, thanks for being you!

For my nephews and nieces Doug, Rachel, Elisa, Dave, Jason, Monica, Matt, Martha, Dan, Karen, Eddie, Tiffany and Nick thank you for keeping the flame aglow.

For their children Gabe, Cameron, Meg, Tracy, Charlotte, Christina, Will, Gabriel and Michelle thank you for continuing our journey.

For my children Jim, Shawna, Kevin, Jen, Ryan and Kaitlin, words cannot express the love, appreciation and gratitude that I hold so close to my heart for allowing me to be a part of your walk and seeing it grow better and better with each passing day because you share yours with Mom and me.

For my grandchildren Julia and Luke, thank you for allowing me to see in you, our hopes and dreams and the very best part of our family's legacy.

For the people of our block, Memory Lane, who started as strangers but became family, friends and life long memories.

Finally and most significantly, for the one person who has taught me that when you believe what you already have is the best, it truly can become much better. I am in debt to my loving wife, life partner, and absolute best friend, my wife Christine. Meeting and falling in love with you my dear, is by far the most significant accomplishment and dream come true that I could ever have imagined. I am forever grateful. This book is for you as we share the rest of our life's journey together!

My Love, My Wife, My Life
Thank you for being you…..

Reflection and Appreciation

I have always had a dream of writing a book and started multiple projects only to start another unfinished work. In 2005, I had a conversation with my children, their spouses and a good friend, Joanne Brooks West, about my writings. Joanne strongly pushed me to complete one work, "until it is done." This then became my project. Joanne has also been most helpful in editing the Final Proof. Thanks Joanne!

The majority of the composition has been written in an airplane as I travel the world for my job in global sales. It has been written over the Atlantic, the Pacific, in Asia, Europe, Latin America and all over the USA. My children Kaitlin and Ryan would fill my IPod with mood music, so I could close my eyes to the outside world and put myself back in time over 50 years ago to being a child on our block up to our last walk, which this describes. At times turbulence was the only thing that could break my mindset.

Throughout my writing of this journal, I have been most fortunate to have my wife Chris read it a number of times to provide her insight.

Kaitlin became my personal editor, proofreading it for grammar, insuring what I wrote made sense! And for her dear friend Alyssa De La Torre for her comments, support and help with the cover photo. For her beloved Grandmother, Connie De Setto, (may she rest in peace), for reviewing the early manuscripts to insure there were no errors in the era I tried to capture.

To my very good friends: Fred Emken, John Brolly, and Deborah and John Aquino for their tremendous support and help in the long process. I am ever so thankful!

Dick did my very first proof read and edited many, many versions, offering continuous support in so many ways. Deb never stopped giving me ideas; I can.t wait for her sequel! Jerry aided me with many concepts, but he will still deny The Pin! If this makes it to Audio Book status, I would love for Jerry to be our reader.

My cousins Eleanor, Marj and Barbara supported my efforts with encouragement and shared many, many memories.

My nephew Doug motivated me throughout the entire process and helped create the title and much more. His son Gabe's valor has inspired me throughout this recollection.

A special thanks to Paul Cassone for allowing me to use his beautiful song: "Here's To Good Friends" to wrap up the journey.

My kids and Chris pushed me to finish it.

I thank you all.

OUR 'VISITS'

Family Photo
The six of us celebrating Dad's Surprise 65th Birthday Party!
1980

THE OPENING

AAAADDDAAAAAAMMMMM!!!!

It was 6:00 P.M., Tuesday, July 21, 1959...Mr. Gates bellowing dinner call, combined with Mr. Murray's piercing human whistle and our blasting Williston Park Fire Alarm at 6 P.M. all came at once...advising all of the 87 kids on Memory Lane that it was time to pack up our baseball gloves, the sawed off broomsticks and our one and only once pink spaldeen and head back to our individual homes to have dinner.

Amazingly, every night, the same thing! Our block would go from a mass bedlam of summer games such as stickball, I Declare War, Steal the Flag, etc to quiet dinner time inside the happy confines of the 42 homes on our beloved block. That's not to mention the two side streets (Leo and Macrame) where other kids lived as well. Shortly after dinner, our block once again transgressed to become a nightly street fair of kickball, punchball, ring around the rosie or hide and seek in the short course of only 55 minutes because by 7 P.M., we were all outside running around again.

We, the Baumbach kids, were proud products of this joy!

THAT EERIE NIGHT IN OCTOBER 2000

October 2, 2000, a year before the tragedy of 9-11, Mom was 83, a month short of her 84th birthday when she went to the fridge to get a glass of juice to help swallow one of her many prescriptions…she made it to the door, opened it and suddenly………she was gone.

Sometime later, after endless unanswered phone calls, I found her lying in a quite peaceful state, the refrigerator door open, and glass in her hand. I hopelessly tried CPR, all the while thinking it was to no avail…. why hadn't I come earlier? Why hadn't I stopped staining my deck? I ran to Mom's yellow kitchen wall phone, and made the worst calls of my life. First to my wife Chris, for comfort, consolation and guidance. Then to Mom's beloved St. Aidan's parish rectory; (I knew Mom would want a priest there to guide her and us!); my brothers Dick, Jerry and our sister Deb and…the police…I assumed that what was what one was supposed to do when they walk into a house and find a body gone but a soul vibrantly still alive, hovering above and taking this all in from a very different view.

What I had seen in movies, was now taking place in front of me. None of it seemed real.

In many ways, as Jerry said, it was truly my fortune, to find Mom in this state. We were alone, Mom and I; having our own private time to say goodbye, with me looking lovingly at the woman who gave me life, but who now lay helplessly on her kitchen floor.

A floor? Not really. Rather Mom's personal heavenly launching pad!

Mom was blessed, and as she passed through whatever it is we enter as we leave this earthly world to go to God's haven in heaven, I was in a very strange way somewhat happy. Happy because Mom was back with our Dad!

Dad, a man who left us physically eight years earlier, but due to the cruelties of a tormenting, draining disease called Alzheimer's, Dad, and our family, endured a long 15-year living wake.

Now in the span of a few minutes, they were together again, each wrapped with the love of their life. I felt so good for Dad, for he so loved Mom and I was certain he was reaching out with all of his strength to bring her home to him. Luckily, for Mom's sake, she didn't know she was leaving – she simply did not intend on dying, so, as we told all of her friends, when they meet her again, please don't tell her she left us, this wasn't in **her** plans! She thought she would live to be

100! Her never-ending goal was to live life to its fullest and she tried her best to accomplish that goal.

This recollection is not a sad story, rather it is meant to be a happy reflection. It is a long walk backwards, with many steps forward.

It is a view of the people we knew and the life that existed for so many years for so many people on our Memory Lane in the quant and lovely village of Williston Park, in the 50's, 60's, 70's and onward as four siblings, along with their spouses and children, embarked on our 'Last Walk On Our Block.'

Perhaps a bit of an explanation is in order. We had Mom's funeral, a true celebration of her life, and it was just the way she wanted it. It was a most loving experience for her four children, their spouses, her 11 grandchildren, their spouses and three (now nine) great grandchildren, not to mention her countless friends, relatives, church and senior buddies.

When it was over, Jerry and I spent an amazing amount of wonderful cherished hours going through so many years of memories, furniture, Christmas decorations, clothing, pictures, books, receipts, bank statements, knick knacks, whatever, in Mom's home.

We were most thankful to our wives, Elaine and Chris, for night after night the two of us would gather at Mom's to sort through her life's fortunes because the clock was ticking. We had to close her house for good in less than a month. I really enjoyed that time with Jerry, alone with Mom and Dad's memories. Deb and Dick, due to their living a distance apart, surely missed out.

It is certainly odd, how life can be so busy, but when something like this happens, one always seems to find the time. We had our ups and downs, including what Jerry fondly called, our 'Hummel Wars' as we divided Mom's beloved Hummels throughout the family. They are now spread throughout the country in many homes.

One of Our Family Photo's that Mom and Dad loved.
It's still in my office!
All of their children and their then Grandchildren
e 1980

THE GATHERING

It was Sunday, October 29th; a month after Mom's final rent payment was made, meaning it would bring her home to a close. So we gathered together again, <u>all of us</u>, (Dick and Deb had moved out of state years earlier, but they came back with their families) to make one last visit to Mom's home. While this was not the home we grew up in, it was still our family block; our childhood home was still only 13 doors away. In an odd twist, that was so much our Mom, she sold our home 10 years earlier to the people she ended up renting this home from, on the very same block.

She always eyed this particular house and wanted to rent it when it became available. Mom jumped, all 120 pounds of her, cane in hand, she leaped at the opportunity to move back to her street, our street – back home to her beloved Memory Lane.

So here we were, the home was finally cleaned out and we were bringing the last of the boxes to Goodwill or to Deb's car to send off to Maryland. (How she stored all that stuff we will never know!) Suddenly one of us had a thought. Thinking back, perhaps we will all take credit for it, but I believe it was Dick, who with Mom's passing was given the mantle of Family Leader, who said "why don't we take a walk down the block for one last time, all four of us together." We thought about it for a New York second; magically all siblings quickly agreed. So we did.

A month before Mom passed away; she gave me my birthday gift. She said she couldn't get out to shop, but knew I always cherished this blue dog and her Laurel and Hardy salt and pepper shakers which were in our home for years. I remember her hugging me and crying as we shed some tears when I opened the wrapping.

I wonder if she sensed she would soon be leaving us.

OUR LAST WALK ON OUR BLOCK

Williston Park is a town where every child deserved to have grown up. Situated on Long Island, it is a relatively short distance from the hustle and bustle of the Big City but it has the ever loving charm of small town USA. Caring neighbors, friendly shopkeepers, civic minded citizens, dedicated politicians, countless volunteers, it is a hamlet that could be the set for many a movie about the 'good life' in middle America. Williston Park is an America where love of neighbor is not only preached but practiced.

Our block, Memory Lane, is not large. It is bordered on the west by Koch Boulevard, though we never thought of it as a Boulevard, since that was too long a word and we couldn't spell it anyway! Our block is intersected in the center by Macramé Place and Leo Place (both small blocks) and at the east by Maximus Road (a rather large street) and it ends on the east as a dead end, just east of Wallington Road. Get the picture? Mom's 'new house' was on the 'Eastern End' of the block.

Initially, as we started our walk, Dick, Jerry, Deb and I (Ron) went alone. We turned to our right, as there was no reason to go to the two homes to the left since we had no idea who these people were now nor then. In fact, Mom didn't say much about her 'new' next door neighbor on the left, and frankly, we had never really ventured that far on the block as kids anyway. Basically, with the exception of Jerry dating his first real love, way back in prehistoric time, we didn't really travel to this part of our block. We probably weren't allowed to go that far!

We paused by the home on the right, next to Mom's home, we had no knowledge of these people either and therefore we had nothing to say, hmmm, this may be a very short walk!

Dick returns from Army basic training in 1965, prior to heading to Ohio and then Korea. We had to all stand up straight or perhaps get enlisted. We also wore these clothes on Sundays for church and dinner. Please Note: We didn't dress this way for Our Walk!

THE FAYS

Initially, our idea seemed kind of strange. Our thoughts were held to ourselves since we really didn't know any of these people, or most of those who lived on this particular section of the block, except that is, for the house two doors away from Mom. It belonged to Vincent and Linda Fay.

Vincent was the son of Mom and Dad's very good friends, Roger and Nora Fay. Both Roger and Vincent were elected Mayors of our Village. I always thought that Dad was the most important reason Mr. Fay continually was re-elected!

Before electronic media wonders such as Facebook and Twitter helped to win elections, there was the simple stuffing of envelopes and door to door flier delivery.

Dad would 'volunteer' us to go door to door placing their campaign ads in mailboxes or on front stoops. (Sometime while doing this we were told we couldn't place them inside the mailboxes as they were for mail only....I was afraid I would get carried away by the postal police!)

I remember I was paid a penny an ad. I didn't get rich, but enjoyed the civic pride Dad felt in helping his very good friend Roger win repeated elections. And I never knew exactly who it was who laid out the money for my labor – Dad or The Committee?

The Fays and the Baumbachs met through their mutual membership in the Williston Park Fire Department and Auxiliary. On Memorial Day and July 4th, they would march in the town parades. Dad proudly wore his fireman uniform. Or he would march with the Williston Park Little League Teams that Dad coached. Dad enjoyed coaching the Farm Team or Minors, because these kids were more eager to learn as opposed to being 'stars.' So he didn't coach the older, more experienced players. Teams were named for local sponsors, such as the Vamps for the Fire Department, or Meadowbrook Bankers for the local bank. No teams went by major league baseball team names such as the Yankees, Dodgers or Giants. In fact there were only 16 teams then and my Mets were years away from being born. If you wore a team logo cap or jacket you would stand out, you had to be rich!

The Fays had two daughters and three sons. Vincent was a year younger than me and he became one of my childhood friends. In essence their family of seven pretty well matched up to our family of six.

When we were younger we would visit the Fays on Broad Street. I remembered their basement and thought it was so large because I always got lost there or maybe it was because I could never find my way out of their closet. Truth be told, the basement was quite small, as was my perspective!

Sadly Vincent passed away of a heart attack a few years back and his widow Linda and their children still lived' in their home. Luckily, Linda would look in after Mom. We talked about how Mr. Fay (somehow, even as three of us had already marched into our 50's, we still called our parents' friends Mr. and Mrs.) surprised Mom and Dad on their 40th Wedding Anniversary party and picked them up in his classic 1929 Ford Model T. How proud they looked as he drove them to their surprise party at Edmond's Showcase Restaurant in Garden City. I recalled Dad's face beaming. He deserved it; little did we know then that his memory was already fading away.

And we proudly reflected on the day Mr. Fay came to our home in 1958 and took 'The Picture.' It is a photo of the four of us on our stairway. He must have taken over 100 poses. But this picture is a classic. The picture we all cherish and still show to this day.

Mr. Fay was the kind of man who got things done. He was a most cherished part of our parents' lives. We agreed on the meaning and value of their friendship and each of us silently thanked him and his wife, Nora, for all that they meant to our family for so many years.

The Fays taught me Civic Pride ......and we walked on....

The Picture
Deb, Ron, Jerry, Dick

THE TREEMANS

We crossed Maximus Road, or simply Maximus as the natives would say, and right in front of us was the Treeman's house. We didn't have a clue who may have lived there currently, but to us it was the Treemans. It was a light tan house, located on the corner, with the entrance on Memory Lane but with their garage towards the back with the driveway facing Maximus Road. They had a lot of kids. We tried to remember the names and how many there were. Perhaps there were ten. I befriended Stuart, their eldest years earlier and he, along with another friend, whom you will meet later, and I created our own version of the Three Stooges. I was chosen to be Curly. Maybe we knew the future of my gorgeous hairline!

Stuart, Scott and I even talked Stuart's Dad, Frank Treeman into letting us build a clubhouse behind their garage. It was so cool, but not in a temperature control way... since we had one major problem...it had no ventilation. When we closed our roof/hatch it became sweltering hot.

Once, when we played in it, one of the other two explorers appeared to get deathly ill, but lived to mightily talk about it bravely the next day.

I recalled how we made our own business – a local street newspaper – the Memory Lane News – we only sold a few copies, probably because I argued that we should charge a nickel and who in their right mind would pay a nickel in 1960 to a bunch of 11 year olds attempting to publish a paper. But it was the first and only paper our block ever had!

We also did a puppet show in their backyard, for which we also foolishly charged admission. It lasted one show and even then we had to let in a bunch of freebies to fill the seats! But it was an outstanding show! The reviews were awesome.

Prior to 1969, and the first manned landing on the Moon; prior to Alan Shephard who became the first American in space; right after that Russian fellow named Yuri Gagarin (but the Russians didn't compare to an American in the 1950-60's), the real scientist of note, in our mind was Stuart, our Memory Lane Scientist and he was only about eleven.

In a complementary way, Stuart's face somewhat resembled the current NBA star Dirk Nowitzki, yet he also looked a little like a young version of 'Doc' from 'Back to The Future' fame. He would creatively think about how we could someday 'launch' ourselves into space. We would go to our favorite baseball field, commonly called the 'Lots' and attempt to venture into our own space journey.

One long summer, after a series of many failed attempts, I recalled we successfully sent a frog on a space mission that seemed to go way up into the sky. It actually did explode off of our makeshift launch pad and it took off and sailed high into the sky, only to come back about a hundred yards from our own Cape Canaveral.

As we found our space capsule, we then searched for our passenger. The very first Astro Frog! Perhaps he escaped into space, because we never found him. Hopefully he is still orbiting, but as maturity and good conscience have peacefully settled in years later, I think we regretfully realized we did him in, in a most cruel way. Sorry Astro!

The Treemans probably had an equal amount of boys and girls. Testing our memories we recalled only a few: Stuart, Rebecca, whom I didn't have many memories of except for having to go to their house once during one of our block parties to talk her into coming out for the festivities, and it worked; (what charm I possessed!), Rosa, Maria (who would re-appear in our life years later as the mother of one of my son Ryan's High School and College Basketball teammates), and a number of others!

As I told my stories to Dick, Jerry and Deb, they must have gotten bored silly, or maybe Dick simply turned off his hearing aid, which was basically the same reaction they had to my stories when we were all young. Some things never change, do they?

We all reflected about how wonderful a friend Jean Treeman was to Mom. How she would come down the block in the evening and sit with our beloved Mrs. Burke, who was a most instrumental player on our block, and Mom on our front stoop – every summer evening.

For some reason, all the neighborhood parents

seemed to gather at our stoop, the Burke's stoop or the Murray's stoop every night! If you don't know what a stoop is, that's sadly your loss. A simple explanation: it was the entrance to our homes and was built with bricks. You could play stoop ball either alone or against another by throwing the ball against various steps and trying to get it past your opponent. If you made it across the street on a fly, it was a home run!

Stoops seemed to cool the temperatures on those hot summer evenings. Everyone had their own summer lawn chairs which would be carried throughout the block in search of the nightly gathering by someone's stoop.

No one had air conditioning; in fact, no one could envision air conditioning being installed in a home. The only place you could get a sense as to what air conditioning was, would be if you went to the new Grand Union Food Store. The A&P didn't even get A/C till years later. I remembered going to the A&P with Dad on our weekly Friday shopping rounds and freezing when they finally modernized that store. Even the sawdust wooden floors went the way of modern day linoleum in the 1960's.

So instead of the wonders of air conditioning, we survived with fans; placed our hands in cold water; or rubbed an ice cube on our wrists, like our Uncle Eddie used to tell us to do. Sometimes you even got invited to go to the Howe's or the Garrett's backyard pools. These was not the kind of pools one buys today, rather they were the plastic blow up 1-½ feet deep ones, but they felt so good when you jumped in and splashed each other! Never a need for a lifeguard; just a bathing suit and usually a hose, because the water seemed to come out as fast as it went in!

Regretfully, one of the Treeman daughters passed away in a car accident – Rebecca got hit and was gone. Another daughter, Rosa, sadly never woke up from her sleep.

While we stood in front of their home, it seemed so quiet, versus what it was like for years gone by... but their memories lived on inside.

But Who Was Charlie Ox?

Dad was not really into the sciences, except when it came to cb radios. He would have a ball talking to all these new 'friends' and making up funny stories about who he was and whom they were. Everyone was called Charlie Ox. We had no idea who Charlie was, or what he looked like, but that was the name Dad always used if he didn't know someone's name. Cool handle:
"10-4, Charlie Ox, Over and Out."

The Treemans taught me Imagination. And our walk continued....

THE FOGARTYS

Our next home was the Fogarty's. They appeared to be the perfect couple. A handsome Dad, a pretty Mom, two cute girls, Rosemary and Elizabeth, (the latter was a friend of Deb's), a station wagon and of course a house in the country on Memory Lane. Sort of like a Personal Pleasantville in Williston Park.

We didn't know too much about them, except that Mom always spoke fondly of them. For all we knew, Mr. Fogarty could have been a member of the CIA or perhaps the Russian Embassy! But we would never have known that, because if Mom didn't like someone, she wouldn't talk negative about them, she would simply say something like, 'some things are best left unsaid,' or 'if you have nothing nice to say about someone, say nothing at all' and my personal favorite: "Someone told me

something about so and so, but I can't tell you."
That one always drove me crazy!

We never knew who so and so was, or what was
the something that happened and never ever
knew who the someone was who started this
entire chain of who said what that we couldn't
know.

Suddenly the Fogartys were gone, moved away.
Perhaps an alien spaceship took them to a far
away planet. Perhaps Rod Sterling, through the
magic of Twilight Zone, had us imagine their
presence and they never ever were there in the
first place. Or maybe they were simply reassigned
by the CIA.

Whatever it was that caused them to leave, we
never knew because they were suddenly gone,
away, packed up and oddly forgotten!

We also never really knew who moved into their
house, and for some odd reason, we never seemed
to give it a second thought either.

Until years later, when Chris and I happened to go
to Mass at St. Aidan's and we sat in a pew next to
a relatively young woman, who stopped us after
Mass, saying she recognized Chris.

She knew Chris from working together at North
Shore Hospital. In a weird twist, it turned out she

had just moved out of the Fogarty house on our very own Memory Lane.

During our conversation, she mentioned it was her understanding that the house was always occupied by girls. But the weirdest twist was that she had then moved to Broad Street which was the same street Mom had moved to, regretfully, for a very short time in between her 40 years of living on Memory Lane! She never liked being away from her block.

Pretty girls –Faded Away – Pretty much forgotten

Spooky or Surreal?

While the family all gathered to plan for Mom's wake, we had a number of opinions as to the exact dress Mom had told each of us that she wanted to be buried in. We struggled and had a problem finding all of the dresses, except for one, from Chris and my wedding, hanging in her closet. Where were the other dresses? We called a number of dry cleaners, thinking they would have one with her name on it, to solve our problem. No luck. So we finally had to make a decision and chose this particular pink dress. At dinner, the first night of her viewing, we all went back to Mom's house for dinner.

The question arose again about 'the dress,' when suddenly, as Elisa, Dick's daughter, reached under the kitchen sink to pull out the box containing the kitchen trash bags, we all saw a little piece of paper fly out of the box, rose to the ceiling and came floating down. We thought it was trash, stuck in the carton. When Elisa picked it up and looked at it, she let out a shriek. It was a very tiny one inch picture of Mom, from our wedding, wearing the chosen pink dress! Problem solved! Thanks Mom!

The Fogartys taught me Curiosity.

And we walked about 25 feet next door....

Dad, Jerry and Matt... also curious!

THE VIGGIANIS

Moving along we next came to the Viggiani family home. The parents were Russ and Nadene, their son was Russ and their daughter was named Donna. The Viggianis were friends of Mom and Dad, we could tell because we saw home movies of them at Mom and Dad's gala annual New Year's Eve Parties having a grand time!

For reasons many kids don't understand but parents clearly do, we always had to remain upstairs during these parties. It always seemed pretty noisy in our finished basement as the New Year would come rolling in and Dad, a relatively quiet man, became the Party Guy. In fact, one year he dressed up as the New Year's Eve Baby while another friend dressed as Old Man Time. There were pictures; there were Super Eight Movie films.

There were also lamp shades that made it from their normal position on end tables into the movies as well…. mmmm, I suddenly can hear Mom telling me to 'stop writing about this and change the subject!'

As it was, the Viggianis were our Italian neighbors on a block full of Irish and Germans ancestries. I believe they were truly one of the few Italians on our block, which was amazing considering the demographics for the area in this period of time.

Jerry tends bar to Ron – after the real party e 1958

They were cool folks and years later I made a sales call on Mr. Viggiani at his job at Fairchild Republic. Talk about a weird feeling. Here I was, a kid making a sales call on my neighbor! Unfortunately, I was way too wet behind the ears in sales at that time to have it help me get the business. Even with all the aid Mr. Viggiani tried to give me, I failed to get the sale!

The four of us spoke about them being very friendly folk. Rusty was close to Jerry's age and was a pretty good athlete. Back then, Rusty looked a bit like Ricky Nelson from Ozzie and Harriet. Donna, his sister, was a little younger, but older than me and would rank with her next door neighbors, the forgotten Fogarty girls, in terms of Memory Lane Heartthrobs back then, with no offense to Deb, but sisters don't count!

Day Trips and Vacations!

Growing up with Dad, we often heard of his displeasure for his daily commute to and from his job in Flushing. It was not a venture Dad enjoyed; he really had a hatred of traffic. He worked from 5 AM to 3 P.M. and would arrive home about 3:45 every day. He had a rotating shift, with Saturday being a constant day off, so every seventh weekend it meant Dad was home with us on a full Sunday. It also meant that he would have a weekday off every week, which was sort of cool, because on some of those hot summer days, he would take us to Bar Beach - we rarely went to Jones Beach – I never knew why, but we always went to our town beach on the North Shore of Long Island, on the Sound, with the hard rocks when the tide was out, and the pebbly sand when the tide was in, but it was our Bar Beach!

It had a cool playground, a refreshing snack bar, and a black topped parking lot that would burn the soles of our feet, since no one wore sandals or flip flops then. We wore sneakers, and you wouldn't want to put your sand coated feet in them on the way back to the car.

Bar Beach became a family haven for us on those hot sunny summer days, and while we didn't go as often as we would have liked, when we did, however, we appreciated the surprise trip.

My most vivid and shared memories of those family beach outings were two:

One rather scorching weekday, our whole family set off to Bar Beach. I brought a beach ball with me, which I really took a liking to. Somehow, it got caught in the current and started floating out to sea. Dick, ever the risk taker, decided to be the hero to his youngest brother and started swimming out in the deep water to rescue it. Dad looked up and saw this and saw the currents and saw danger. So Dad immediately swam out to Dick and brought him back to shore. I remember standing there watching this scene and thinking, Wow! Dad is going to be mad at Dick!

Interestingly, when they both returned and after they caught their collective breaths, all I remembered hearing was Dad telling Dick – "Why would you do that? Why would you do that? Why would you do that? I can always buy Ronald another ball, but I can't replace you."

A few years later, another event occurred, not quite as dramatic, but pretty awe-inspiring, at least for me. That week Jerry received his St. Aidan's Grammar School Ring. We would get these platinum finger treasures in the eighth grade. They probably cost a small fortune. Well, as we were on another outing to Bar Beach and somehow in the course of horsing around and playing in the sand, Jerry noticed that his new ring was missing. He looked everywhere. It was like 'who took my ring?' Mom and Dad were not too happy: 'How could you lose it? Where did you put it last? Why did you take it off? How could this happen? Yada, Yada, Yada.'

As this was going around, I remembered thinking that St. Anthony was the Patron Saint for Missing Things, that's probably not his official title, so to the purists, I apologize. Anyway, I decided to go to Dear St. Anthony and pray, asking him to help us find Jerry's ring. Well, as I finished my prayers, I bent down in the sand and started to sift through it with my fingers, within seconds I found the ring. I was so excited. St. Anthony and me, we found the ring!

The joy most likely lasted only a few seconds because it was probably followed with: 'Ronald, why did you hide the ring?'

Our vacations were normally quite simple, but fun. We would usually go to Aunt Rose's in Albany and stay for a number of days and explore the wonders of upstate New York. As we got a little older, we would go to family vacation spots and stay in cozy hotel rooms, with lakes or pools nearby. One year we drove to visit Mom's brother, our Uncle John and his family. He had been convalescing from polio in his home in Cincinnati, Ohio. It was during a period when Dad's job was in jeopardy since the Jane Parker A&P bakery employees were in a long protracted strike. Staying in small family motels along the way, the ride there was great. Deb stood the entire way in the middle of the front seat looking back and talking to Dick, Jerry and me. No one ever knew that this would someday be so unsafe. Seat belts? Car Seats? They didn't come along for many a year later.

The ride back, however, was a disaster. As we drove through West Virginia, our car stalled and something with the engine went kerplunck. We had to go to some car repair shop and stay the evening in some small town. But we were all together, had a fun time, and got to see America and I for one, truly enjoyed the family bonding we shared. This was Dad at his best. Nothing would dare to hurt his family and he made sure we somehow someway would still have fun.

The Viggianis taught me Trust and we walked next door...

Deb, enjoying a family picnic at Aunt Roses e 1959

THE O'REILLYS

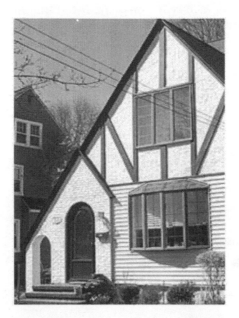

The O'Reilly house was next – they lived in the light brown house with a darker brown trim, a trim that never seemed to change, it was an odd sort of brown coloring, not very colorful. With all attempts not to be sarcastic, it was somewhat reflective of our view of the O'Reillys – very nice people, but quiet and very unassuming, you might say low key before low key was called low key.

Stories were abound about Mr. O'Reilly – he was a big strong strapping man – sort of a gentle giant, quiet, and perhaps the king of, well the king of low key.

Born in Ireland, supposedly he was a national boxing champion there and the rumors were that he once lost a fight to Joe Louis, The Joe Louis. This kept a lot of us in awe of him and his son Timmy – who was about a year or so younger than me, but who also had strong likenesses to his Dad. He was powerful beyond his years! No one ever messed with Timmy.

Timmy would occasionally play baseball with us and I vividly recalled playing our typical summer evening baseball game in the 'lots' behind Wilson Boulevard. As the sun was setting, it became harder and harder to see the ball. We used to do fungo in those days, but if we felt brave enough we would also go with 'live pitching.' Perhaps the best arm of the day belonged to our family lefty, Jerry. Jerry could throw the ball faster than anyone I had seen. And when he threw the ball up in the air, it went so high; you could tie your shoelaces and still have time to catch it!

The opposite was fungo, for those who may not know, this is when the batter throws the ball up in the air and hits it himself without the aid of pitcher throwing him the ball.

This one night Timmy was up and I was playing

shortstop. He started to hit some line drive balls that came straight at me. The only problem was I could not see them, but I could *hear* them as they went whizzing by. That was it, 'Game called, we're outta here!' I yelled. Freakin' frightful! That O'Reilly boy could hit!

Once, when we were playing stickball in the street, and home plate was in front of the O'Reilly house, I was at bat. I loved stickball but every year, for some reason, I always had a two week slump and could not hit the broad side of a barn, not that we had barns in our neighborhood to hit. I did manage however, to hit the O'Reilly house. Unfortunately, as I swung my broomstick bat, the bat flew out of my hands and went straight for the middle two windows in the front of their house. Everyone stood and watched the path of the bat. It was such a beautiful sight seeing this flying bat soaring in the air. SMACK, it hit the window with a bang, but hit it solidly along the entire length of the bat, and not either end. I couldn't have planned it better. The sounds we heard were of solid glass being hit by solid wood, but no broken glass. Kids being kids, the game ended and everyone ran home. It was clearly the best hit I never had!

Timmy had a younger brother named Kenneth. Timmy was darker skinned with brown hair, and Kenneth was platinum blond with curly hair. Those Irish genes were strong!

We didn't recall then and I don't recall much now about Kenneth, he was somewhere in between Deb's age and mine, but we never knew too much about him, then or now, perhaps he was standing behind the window when my bat hit it and it scared the daylights out of him!

Their mom, Mrs. O'Reilly, was a friend of Mom's – remember she was Irish – and that was sort of like a magnet to Mom. Mom had her as one of her 'walk down the block to say hello' friends. Oddly, I don't recall Mrs. O'Reilly ever coming to our home, maybe it was the German influence from Dad, which basically existed in name only, because Dad became more Irish than most of Ireland's countrymen, especially with his famous version of 'When Irish Eyes Are Smiling' which he sang most lovingly throughout his Alzheimer years. Dad bought more Irish records than any other, with the possible exception of Mitch Miller and his crazy bouncing ball. But when all was said and done, we still never recalled Mrs. O'Reilly ever coming to our house to visit. I bet it was that window!

The O'Reillys taught me the meaning of Strength. We then walked a few steps to the left…

THE MCADAMS

We continued walking, about 30 steps to the home that housed the man who gave our family a new meaning to the word 'Pinhead.' He lived in the deep green house next door to the O'Reillys along with his bevy of kids, both guys and gals. The McAdams – Ruth and Hugh. Oh we used to have so much fun with the name Hugh – 'who, you, no its Hugh!' 'Who's calling, it's Hugh? Who? Hugh? Who? Who's Hugh'?

Anyway, one day, and I forget the actual context of what caused it, but Mr. McAdams was referring to one of us about his neighbors on our end of the block and his reference was something like 'those pinheads.' We thought it was funny and later on realized it was also a bit sarcastic, but maybe he was just getting back at us for all the years of the 'Hugh – You' jokes we did, supposedly behind his back.

One of my memories of Mr. McAdams, which became sort of a true confession, was the day that Scott Murray and I were at Mass together. We found ourselves in the pew directly behind Mr. Hugh McAdams. During this particular Mass we did a lot of kneeling, standing, kneeling, sitting and kneeling. Whatever I had had for lunch got the better of me and I ripped a loud uncontrollable fart. Scott openly looked at me as if to say, "Wow, who did that"? I looked back at him, pointed at Mr. McAdams and nodded my head as if to say, "he's the culprit." We both giggled and laughed, which caused some additional external explosions. I guess I said Hugh did it!

Mr. McAdams looked like Robert Young, the actor famous for the TV shows "Father Knows Best" and "Dr. Quigley" the trusted family physician. He was a striking handsome man. All kidding aside, they were truly nice people and really liked Mom and Dad.

They had a bunch of kids Dick's age, some a little older, many a bit younger.... one was near my age named Jack, who pursued but failed in his attempts to date our cousin, Eleanor. She was one of our three very pretty female cousins who lived around the corner, in our neighborhood, but back then it seemed odd, at least to me, to have a friend try to date your close relative.

Most of our memory talk in front of their home

was from Dick talking about how all their kids always looked so cool. In the days of American Graffiti and Happy Days they were our very own Fonzie Family! And our Dick fit right in with them.

Years later Mrs. McAdams gave Mom their huge artificial Christmas Tree – it was spectacular; it was also incredibly large, so much so had New York City taken artificial trees it could have been positioned in Rockefeller Center! It was so large, that Santa could put gifts under it and it would be three days before anyone on our block would find them all! Mom took it, nurtured it, preserved it, somehow stored it and in a weird way, it ended up in Chris and my house and lasted there for years until we went 'natural' with our own live Christmas Tree Tradition.

The McAdams taught me Confidence and walk on we did......

THE WEBERS

Next we moved towards the Weber's House. Another brown home, though a bit lighter shade. It was always very well manicured. The Webers were a quiet couple, perhaps they were society's first 'DINKS' – Double Income, No Kids. That was so very odd back then! Especially on our block. But they did have a special living creature in their home. Her name was Gracie.

Gracie was a dog, a cute little terrier that had her own room, and in essence was a human being in a dog's body. She, along with Mr. & Mrs. Weber completed the Weber family. We never knew if Mr. or Mrs. Weber even had first names, or if they even had jobs. Mysterious people, with a humanistic dog. They were a really nice couple, they were also quite religious.

In addition, they were very good friends of Mom. Hey, why wouldn't they be, after all Mom said her Mother had the same type of dog, which, as the story goes, passed away within a week after Mom's Mom's sudden death on the day she mailed out Mom and Dad's wedding invitations. So it was a very natural link that Mom had with them.

They treated their beloved Gracie as if she was their daughter. They would dress Gracie in real clothes. Remember, this was a time that no one bought pet clothes, never mind dressing their pets in them. Perhaps Mrs. Weber made them, because we didn't have too many pet stores back then, especially ones that sold pet clothing!

Gracie was the best-behaved 'child' on the block. We never saw her poop or pee; perhaps she held it in for 15 years! She may have taken the term 'House Trained' to a different level. The Webers were good folks and often drove Mom to her many Church meetings. We reflected on their being as good a neighbor as one could ask for.

Gracie

Our Pets

We were fortunate to live in a time where it was felt that children needed to have pets. While ours did not seem to last too long, either in life or at our home, at least we tried.

We had our share of all kinds of God's loving creatures:

We had blue parakeets, green parakeets and yellow canaries. We tried numerous times to teach them to talk or sing, but to no avail. We would occasionally, 'free' them for flights through the house, which didn't go well with Mom or Dad. It was always an adventure getting them back in their cage.

Dad would clean the cage, taking out the paper and that gritty sand like stuff that would be on the cage floor. Some of the birds wouldn't mind us petting them, others loved to bite.

Our fish would be in small tanks, large tanks or simply swam in a bowl. They ranged from colorful tropical types to gold fish or guppies, which seemed to reproduce rather well. Cleaning the tank was a task no one enjoyed and it probably led to their early departures.

In fact when the birds or fish would leave, usually

meaning die, we would normally have ceremonies to memorialize them and either do a graveside burial in the backyard or a quick simple flush. Shoeboxes made for great coffins.

Bye Bye!

We also had horned toads, turtles, chameleons, and frogs. I recalled once having caught a bunch of frogs, which I stored in a special jar. Not being too scientific, I didn't then know that the laws of nature required animals to breathe. I left the jar tightly closed in the backyard. One scorching hot summer day upon returning from a visit to a dear friend Mrs. Hearn, I went to see my 'pet frogs.' I was most surprised with what my eyes beheld! Let's just say my frogs probably died on a Fryday!

Sparky was the Murray's dog, we got his brother and forgot his name. He was tan in color and a very cute dog, but had one major problem. He really enjoyed ripping Mom's and our Aunt Estelle's stockings. After a few months, that was the excuse that we were given; he had to go and off he went.

A few years later we were asked to take ownership of a huge beagle named Tiger, who belonged to Dad's boyhood friend who was also our family dentist. The dog was cool, loving and harmless. And he didn't rip stockings. But he didn't quite take to his new home. He would always run away from our house to his old home…running three miles, over railroad tracks, back to our Dentist house. After a series of these trips, we gave him back and he was sent to live on a farm. We heard that he eventually broke loose and came back home – traveling over 100 miles!

We then got a gorgeous collie named Laddie, who was the son of one of our neighbor's, the Garrett's dog, Lady. Lady was a beautiful dog who looked just like Lassie. Everyone loved Lady. She was calm, kind, loved it when anyone would pet her and was a truly stunning animal. Lady had a litter and we were fortunate to be given one of her puppies. I believed Laddie became my dog, or so it seemed as no one really appeared to want him except for me.

I always dreamed of being Timmy from the TV show Lassie. Timmy had his tremendous canine companion who would help him out at all times; be one to share secrets with and would never ever complain. I wanted to name him Lassie, but that was a girl's name, so he became my Laddie.

Laddie and I also shared adventures, as much as any eight year old could. I would pretend we were a horse and buggy team. I would put the leash on Laddie and have him pull me as I rode my bike – until one day he saw another dog and bolted after him. I went faster than I ever could imagine, sort of like Charlton Heston in Ben Hur and eventually crashed to the ground. We stopped doing that trick.

Laddie had behavior issues and as much as we tried, we couldn't properly train him. I remembered the day when I was told we had to give Laddie away to another family. Being that he had a fan club of one, my vote didn't mean much and I recalled standing in the alley way between the Burke's house and ours, all alone crying.

I knew that there had to be more to the story than what I understood to be simple behavior issues because that was not like Mom and Dad. Maybe he tore apart Mom and Estelle's stockings like Sparky's brother or maybe he would always run home to his previous owner as Tiger did. All I knew was we had to give him up and he moved to live with a family who lived around the corner from us on Wallington Road.

I would ride by his new house and looked at those nasty boys who had my Laddie. As time crept on, eventually I started to gradually get over it; perhaps because we only had Laddie for about three months and for all I knew, maybe that was the original plan -- perhaps we were simply training him for these people!

My concern returned on a cold winter night. The home that Laddie moved to caught fire. It was a stupid act. We heard that the stupid boys who lived there hid under their stupid bed and started to play with stupid matches. It was a huge stupid fire. I remembered Dad and all the other firemen on our block running down the street to the fire to meet all of the fire trucks. The night was long and cold and the fine ladies of the auxiliary, the firefighters' spouses, including Mom, were there serving the firefighters coffee all night long. All of us kids ran to the fire and watched the house burn. For me it was most painful. My Laddie lived in that house. All I could imagine was Laddie dying a cruel death in a home that he simply did not belong in. Finally word came out that all the kids, the parents and their pet were safe. I was so relieved, but I stopped making the ride by visits. They almost killed my dog!

Fortunately, because of our walk, I finally learned why we had to give up Laddie. Deb confessed that as a small child, she was very afraid of large dogs.

Our family favorite dog and the one that did stay with us for years, was Cherie, a small, loving black French poodle. Cherie was our Aunt Estelle's dog, but her landlord would not allow pets so we volunteered to take her in. Cherie became a family member and she loved it when Estelle would visit on weekends. Oddly, she never went to our upstairs bedrooms except when Estelle was there and then she would jump up and snuggle with her in bed.

We loved it when Cherie was allowed to have her hair grow out and then she would look like a real dog. But occasionally Mom would have her get a feminine groomer's haircut. When that happened, I was not too fond of being seen walking her. Way too poofie with her pom pom tail and bow on her head. She didn't even smell like a dog!

Cherie stayed very emotionally close to Estelle. Sadly, a week after our Aunt Estelle passed away, Cherie took ill and never recovered. In life, she was a tremendous dog; in death, a great memory.

Our Cherie

The Webers taught me Contentment and we walked the 18 feet next door.

THE KELLEHERS

Next door we came to the dark house with all those deep green bushes all around the house. It was Mayor Kelleher's house.

We never met Mayor Kelleher, but he was famous in our town for being one of our beloved Mayors. Imagine, a politician actually living on our block, the Mayor! They even named the ball field where we played Little League after him – Kelleher Field. He passed away when we were young and we basically only recalled oddball things. One was his widow, Mrs. Kelleher and her large arms and legs, Mom said it was water that caused them to be so big. They were huge! And two was their daughter who always parked her green car in the street. Same spot, all the time.

We had a rule back then, if the ball you hit, hit her car, it was a considered a foul ball. At times we ruled her car our home base for our daily game of

Ring a Leaveio! But you didn't want to hang onto the car too long. We never knew what she would do.

I recalled once making a great catch – an incredible catch - only to turn and tumble into her car...I can still feel the pain.... but the joy of my ESPN moment withstood the pain, like any true athlete! And no, she didn't see or hear about the play! She had no idea I ran into her car, so please don't tell her!

Sitting by the fireplace,
Jerry, Baby Ron and Big brother Dick
e 1951

The Kellehers taught me Honor for the father's commitment to our village. As we turned, we gazed fondly at the homes directly across the street and went 15 feet to our right......

THE SCHATZS

Ah, the Schatzs – Jack Schatz – good old Jack Schatz. Oddly, we never referred to him as Mr. Schatz. He was always – to us at least – Jack Schatz. No one knew his wife's first name. Was it Betty Schatz? Perhaps Sophie Schatz? Who knew, but it was certainly Mrs. Schatz. They also had a son, whom no one really knew...meaning he was older...maybe he hung out with the Kelleher Girl next door! Hmmm....na!

I recalled quite fondly Jack Schatz rushing over to help carry me into our house when I returned from the hospital after being operated on for two spinal fusions due to scoliosis at the age of 15. I came back home on June 1, 1965 after being in bed for six months at St. Charles Hospital.

I had a real problem walking. When Jack saw Mom, Dad, Dick, Jerry and Deb having a problem with me getting out of the car, he ran right over to help pick me up and get me into our house. I will never forget that random act of kindness from a man we didn't know too well but who readily jumped to our aid.   That was really my only memory of him.

The same day we went to my cousin Eleanor's Elementary School Graduation Party. It was a gala affair. I often thought that I inadvertently stole some of her thunder, which I regretted.   The family was thrilled to have me home and when we arrived at the party it was a major celebration.   Obviously for Eleanor and her accomplishments, but in some way also for me. A number of cousins and uncles carried me down their stairs to her finished basement to partake in the festivities. My biggest fear was their dropping me.   They held on tight! The entire experience was a great thrill!

Oh yeah; Jack also had a very nice lawn, which was kind of an odd thing to remember. But at least we were allowed to run on it, unlike another neighbor whose homes we had not reached yet.

The Schatzs eventually moved on. Whether to a final resting place or to another earthly home, we didn't really know. We did recall that there was some sort of issue with some of the folks who moved in afterwards. We didn't quite remember exactly what it was, but there were some issues that appeared to be somewhat negative in nature. Not capable of delving into now, unless of course, our memories get triggered, but remember Mom wouldn't want us talking about these things anyway. Perhaps that's why these memories become sealed in mental / emotional plastic wrap.

Just What is Wax Paper?

Which reminds one of what life was like before scientifically developed plastic wrap.

Ours was a world filled with Wax Paper. It enclosed our sandwiches such as tuna fish (on Fridays), peanut butter and jelly, cream cheese and jelly, cream cheese and olives, cream cheese on date nut bread, cream cheese on canned brown bread, liverwurst, bologna or olive loaf and mustard, etc. The rich kids used Reynolds Wrap Aluminum Foil which served two purposes – one to hermetically seal rich kid's lunches and two to crumble into a ball and toss around the classroom when the nun stepped out of the class room.

Wax paper didn't throw well. But it must have preserved our sandwiches well.

Our classrooms didn't have a cooler or a refrigerator to store lunches. OK, some kids may have had their cool looking Hopalong Cassidy Lunch Boxes with their matching thermos to keep their soup warm, but for the most part, most kids' lunches stayed well preserved in brown bags in the cubby hole under the seat in our desks that also stored our books.

The Schatzs taught me Thoughtful Spontaneity for quickly being there when needed and we walked next door...

Dad's early beginnings, a view of Corona, NY e 1910

THE LABARS

THE MUCERINOS

THE BOOTHS

Now we come to one of those hybrid homes. Once belonged to the Labars and then to the Mucerinos and then to the Booths. Dick led our conversation of the Labars, I would not have recognized them if I walked into them head on, but Dick spun some tales and I leave it to him to expound on them more in follow-up sessions.

My only memory of the Labars was somehow playing on their stoop; they had a really big one, at least for a five year old. It was like a huge wall. I remember sliding off of it and scratching myself on my stomach so bad that it bled, scabbed and bled again. Darn pain lasted for weeks! I always hated that stoop! Ugh, that stinking pain is coming back! It became my personal wall!

Ron and Jerry reviewing a wall of Holy Water
e *1955*

Climbing the Wall

In life we are faced with many walls. They are there every day, and I always believed it is our daily mission to somehow get over our individual daily walls. We simply have to get over those walls.

Some days our wall may seem to be very low, and therefore quite easy to make it over. Other days, perhaps during many stretches in our lives, our walls are quite high and appear to be quite a difficult struggle to climb. But we must go over the wall.

Many times in our lives, we may find we need to go over our wall alone. At other times, we are the ones pulling others over. And at times we are the ones being pulled over. But we must go over that wall.

Our life is a mission of walls, and the last one, the final one, becomes our life's mission to scale it very well!

We will climb the wall!

The Labars sold their home to the Mucerinos, Gabe and Carol. They were an incredibly funny couple, extremely humorous. They had five children. We thought it was three boys and two girls, though we seemed to have forgotten their names and sexes, and had to rely again on Deb's memory for that recollection. They were however, very good loving neighbors.

They created my very first inspiration to get involved in sales. I was a lanky Long Island Press Newspaper carrier, who was not too thrilled with his job, (I hated collecting from my customers and hearing all their excuses why they couldn't pay the $0.45 weekly bill), but Mom said I should go over to see the Mucerinos and ask if they want to buy the paper. I think I was the first neighbor to greet them and I wasn't even bringing a cake or a pie, but a personal hope for a sale. For some reason, she liked me and Mrs. Mucerino agreed to be a new customer and it got me a prize from the Press! It was so cool, my first real sale - ever! And all I had to do was ask for the business….hmmmm, what a novel idea!

During our walk, we talked about them fondly. I recalled my infamous fall from their stoop – must have really affected me, I told you I never forgot that pain, but it happened before the Mucerinos moved in, so they were not to blame!

For many a reason, the Mucerinos continued to be a crucial part of my career. Mr. Mucerino ran his own printing company, which as we were told, became a rather famous restaurant called The Daily Press. He asked me to work for him during my college semester breaks.

When I finally got my first real job as a Sales Representative for Emery Air Freight, I had to make the journey on the Long Island Rail Road from Mineola to Penn Station. I had no idea where I was going or what I should or could expect. It was my very first day and I was a 21 year old rookie. As I was about to board my train, I ran into Mr. Mucerino and he asked me if I wanted to sit with him. We spoke about sales all the way into the city (or I should say, he spoke and I listened). When we finally arrived, I thought we would part our ways, but no, together we took the long escalator ride from the main area of Penn Station to the 34th Street Exit. He continued to give me sales tips all the way up the escalator. I never forgot what that meant to me, an experienced veteran of the sales game helping a rookie on his very first day.

The Mucerinos moved off of the block before they moved off of this world, across the tracks to where we assumed the rich folks lived, to East Williston.

Sadly, he passed away of a heart attack a few years later, followed a few years later by his wife, sort of like when Ricky and Lucy passed on, two really cool people the world missed.

They sold their home to a nice young couple named Booth (Pat and Bob). They also had four children, two sets of Irish twins. Maybe it was the Williston Park water! Bob worked at CBS in New York City. As Mom and Dad aged, they were quite helpful to our parents, putting out their garbage, taking in the empty cans, carrying in groceries, etc. but more importantly they were simply there for them and for us.

I recalled making sales calls to Bob's office in attempts to sell this major account. Since I was older when I met them, I didn't need to call them Mr. and Mrs. Booth, they were simply Bob and Pat.

They too didn't stay on Memory Lane too long, as he received a great job offer from International Paper, which eventually closed down their Manhattan headquarters and had them relocate to the affluent suburbs of Connecticut. Nice to know, but sadly they had to go. As for the sale, yea this time I managed to get it!

The Mucerinos taught me the Value of Humor and we went to a Core Four Home next door....

THE HOWES

We walked next to The Howe house. They lived directly across the street from our house. Dick and Jerry recalled the Patterson family who lived there when we first moved in, but my memory had already forgotten that part, if I ever knew it at all.

Deb and I only remembered the Howes. Mom and Dad knew them well. They were truly part of our Block Core Four: The Howes, The Murrays, The Burkes and The Gates. All were far more like family than neighbors. In fact as you will soon see, some were indeed family, whether by blood or by love.

The Howes had a long relationship with us. Years earlier, when Dad first started working in the A&P he befriended an older gentleman named Ted Cook. Mr. Cook had a newlywed daughter, who was looking to buy a home. Dad told them about one on our block, directly across the street from us. So Heather and Ted Howe bought it, moved in and started to fill their house with kids. This made them another of the very good Catholic families who procreated our block.

The Cooks would visit the Howe's often, and Mom and Dad would visit them as well. We recalled Mrs. Howe's sister who was also a frequent guest, and also quite pleasant. Her name was Ginny. Ironic twists, we had our Aunt Estelle, they had their Aunt Ginny. Both fun loving aunts.

The sadness of the passing of the Cook's was only exceeded by the stories of the sudden death of Mrs. Howe's brother, who if I recalled correctly was a Navy Pilot in WWII. From what we had heard, while in battle, his plane went down at sea. A true war hero we never knew but who gave his all for all of us.

The Howes were great people to us and it truly was a mutual relationship. Mrs. Howe would affectionately call Dad, Hank, not Frank. I never knew what that was all about, but it was taken quite kindly.

Mr. Howe had what some would call, the Irish roast beef face, it was beet red. He looked like one of the lead singers from the Lawrence Welk TV show.

Mr. Howe was also a New York City Fireman, who rose to be a Battalion Chief. We never knew what that meant, but we knew it was very important.

Both of the Howes were always great to the kids on our block. They even invested in one of those infamous blow up pools, the big one that was probably about 1 ½ - 2 feet high. This was BIG back then. They would invite us over on hot days and we would all enjoy the cool waters of their backyard. Awesome!

Ron and Deb e 1958 (I'm the one on the left!)

Their oldest, Harrison, was two years younger than me. I recalled he was a very good athlete, in fact when I was on the disabled list for my spinal surgery from '64 to '65, the stories of lore on Memory Lane were of how Harrison hit a ball <u>over the</u> fence in the 'Lots' which was our baseball, football, and general hang around field a few blocks away. It was our kid haven and generations would go there to play ball. It even had a backstop! Oh how I longed to hit one over that fence, I had come close often, but I never, ever managed to do it! I would wonder, when I was sick, if, once I came back to action, if I could swing one more time for the fences. While I did return to play, in a far more limited role, the ball unfortunately never quite made it over that fence. I believe Harrison still holds that record! Probably forever!

One day a few of us, including Harrison and me, climbed it all the way to the top of the Lots backstop. Some ornery security guard came by and read us the riot act; he took our names and called our parents. We got hell on the field followed by real hell once we all got home. Later on, other kids, who didn't go with us, said, 'why in the world did you give the 'cop' your real names and numbers?' Remember no one carried any sort of 'ID' back then. Ahh, we were simply good kids, we didn't think of trying to beat the system!

Harrison, a very good friend whom I regretfully lost touch with. Sadly, as I finish this tale, Debbie advised that she just learned of his death a few years back. I missed his wake, his funeral, more importantly his adulthood. And I miss my friend Harrison.

He was followed by a sister named Tara, then Connie, Paula, Travis and Jane. Mom and Dad became Paula's Godparents, which was and is a very high honor and for which they were extremely proud. She was always quite special to them.

I recalled Jane, as a young bustling child, would for whatever reason, always call our Dad, Frank. Never Mr.Baumbach, or Mr. B as many kids on the block would call Dad, or Mrs. B for Mom. While sitting in her playpen on their front stoop, she would loudly yell across the street: 'Hiya Frank,' ever so innocently but she never called him Mr. Baumbach. This was very odd back then, because everyone was a Mr. or Mrs. Luckily Dad just laughed, but it made for most interesting dinner conversation because she would do it at the most unusual times, such as when we had friends or relatives visiting, and just as they would come in the house they would hear the child like sounds of 'Hiya Frank' from across the street!

I recalled how Travis, who went to St. John's and desired a sales and marketing career, was recruited by me to be one of my interns for a summer sales program I ran during my days at Emery Air Freight. He did a fantastic job; never shy or afraid of going anywhere for a sale. Whatever success he now has, I hope that I was at least one small part of his foundation!

Coincidently, Mrs. Howe and my Mother-in-law also share the exact same birthday and year. That was always a topic of conversation as I was dating my Chris.

It is also the same birthday as Pope John XXIII, but he was about 50 years older than them! Mom would follow the Howe children's successes, whether it be via marriage or career growth, through her relationship with Mr. and Mrs. Howe, even after the Howes moved away. Years after the passing of both Dad and Mom, we fortunately still correspond with them during the Christmas season. I very much look forward to their cards and handwritten notes.

AFTER THE HOWES

After the Howes moved on they were followed by a lovely couple. While we did not recall their name we did recall two thoughts about them:

1) They became friends with Mom and grew to become one of her many 'volunteers' to drive her to Church.

2) The husband supposedly had a very bad kidney, and was in need of a transplant. The wife donated hers to her husband. They were truly a sharing, caring and loving couple.

> Life is for Giving:
> Be a Donor!

The Howes taught me Dignity and we walked to the Second Core Four Family next door.........

THE MURRAYS

The Murrays were next, another of our Core Four. Their history with our family goes way back, to Mom's childhood. An explanation is therefore in order: Mom's best friend growing up in the Bronx was Amy Herrscher, who had a number of sisters. One was her older sibling Ginger. Ginger was a lovely short woman, quite funny and quick witted, who visited the Murray's often. She reminded me, in a very fond way, of Gracie Allen. I believe she was single. She was also a most beloved visitor to our block. She was a nurse and truly a great representative of her profession – a most caring person. Ever cheerful, ever helpful.

While I was laid up in our home hospital bed during my six month long convalescence from spinal surgery in the mid '60's, Ginger would help Mom tend to me whenever she visited the Murray's. I remembered her changing my endless bandages. She sadly passed away on one of my birthdays and to this day I have kept her prayer card, for she was a very special person. There was also another sister, Miriam, who had a number of children and the youngest sister named Carolyn.

Over the years, Mom kept in touch with Amy, who married a gentleman named Ted Landrith and they had a number of children who were close in age to us boys.

Carolyn and Mom were also friends from their youth as well. Over the course of life's journey, they grew very close, so close that Carolyn was asked to be my Godmother, which occurred three years before we ever moved to Memory Lane.

Years later, when Deb was born, Carolyn's husband, Alex, was asked to be Deb's Godfather. As mentioned, we were close. Enough said!

Our families were very well matched. They had three boys and a girl; we had three boys and a girl. Their Dad drove a bakery truck for Drakes Cakes, our Dad worked for a large bakery - Jane Parker, the A&P bakery. Their Dad was a fireman. Our Dad was a fireman. Their stoop was our stoop, our home was their home.

Dad and Alex became fast friends and both joined the local Williston Park Fire Department, calling themselves 'brothers.' Dad loved Alex, Alex loved Dad. All the kids, when we played on our bikes, go carts or whatever we could move on wheels, wanted to pretend we were firemen, heroically racing off to put out a fire, just like our Dads.

Back when Dad worked for the A&P bakery, Alex was looking for a job and Dad heard of a driver opening at Drakes Cake. Alex took the job, which made all us kids very happy since it meant our families grew up eating Jane Parker apple pies and Drakes Devil Dogs! The pink snow balls were my personal favorite.

For some reason, Dad and Alex had a yearning to become more civic minded and ran for local positions in our town government. Years before polls, campaigns and media attention, (God knows they could have used these tools) they lost to two write in candidates! However, what could have been a negative became a positive. Their friendship grew and while Dad retired early from the fire department, Alex proudly rose to become its Chief.

Alex also would drive his family upstate often for family vacations, similar to what we did. The only difference would be the travel time. What would take us some three-four hours would normally take Alex about an hour and a half. No matter where they went, when we compared times, theirs was always remarkably faster than ours. We assumed they had mastered the art of travel by pneumatic tubes!

Their eldest was Alexander, who was Jerry's age and in the same class at St. Aidan's, our elementary school. Alexander succeeded Dick as the 'Soda Jerk' at Kauder's Soda Shoppe and Stationery (formerly called Como's, though no one knew who the Comos were, or when it exactly became Kauders), I succeeded Alexander; perhaps because I was always being groomed to be a 'Soda Jerk!' Combined, our families had a ten year reign!

For the years that Alexander worked in Kauder's, he would stop at our house every afternoon on his way home, bringing Mom her afternoon copy of the New York Journal American. Mom loved reading newspapers and the Journal American was a classic American Newspaper. I would anxiously await to read the sports section and my then two favorite sports writers – Jimmy Cannon and Barney Kremenko, (both since replaced by a much better sports writer, my son). In season I followed their views of the Met games. In the offseason, I recalled following their scope of the lore of many a young Met phenom who was considered to be rising stars in the Mets Farm System. Unfortunately we didn't have too many players whose stardom kept rising.

Barney Kremenko, however, always intrigued me with his unique writing style. In fact, one of my favorite ballplayers owes his nickname to him. He was the one who donned the famous nickname: 'The Say-Hey Kid' onto Willie Mays.

Alexander's daily visits to our home were never short. Mom loved to chat with Alexander and the two would go on and on talking every afternoon about a myriad of topics. How Alexander got his homework done, I will never know. But those two would often debate at length over the news of the day.

I recalled one strange day, when Alexander was playing some sort of game in the street and he took a terrible fall. Down he went on his arm. It cracked. All the kids heard it. When he got up, it was the most amazing sight we had ever seen at that time. We could actually see the white of his arm bone, or whatever it was called, sticking out of the socket right through his skin! We freaked out and poor Alexander spent the summer on the disabled list with his arm in a large white plaster cast, which everyone, of course had to sign.

Early in life, Alexander had a calling for the priesthood and went on to join the seminary. Our family was thrilled, we would know a priest! I remembered his telling Mom that he couldn't wait to have her come to his confessional. Citing the rule that a priest could not divulge the sins a penitent seeks forgiveness for, he simply said, 'don't worry Mrs. B, I won't say a thing about your sins, all I want to do is to say out loud from the confessional: 'Mrs. Baumbach, you did WHAT!'".

Eventually, he left the seminary for what became a true labor of love and a true act of giving; I believe he became a teacher.

Sally was next in the order of the Murrays. Born between Jerry and myself, she was perhaps our best female athlete on the block, though if I had to choose, Deb would get my vote. My best memory of Sally was sitting on their steps playing board games, such as "Go to the Head of the Class." Whatever the reason, perhaps it was Sally's secret yearning towards teaching but I remembered playing this game with our countless numbers of youthful residents but never recall making it to the actual Head of the Class! Maybe I talked too much! I bet it's because I would distract the 'class' with my impersonation of Lincoln's Gettysburg address as I would recite it word for word.

Scott was next in line, a year younger than me and my best friend growing up. We were the subject of constant comparisons in our youthful rivalry. Contests such as who was taller (always Scott); who could hit a ball farther (me); throw it faster (Scott); longer (Scott) or run quicker (me). We spent countless weekdays playing in his bottomless sand box in the back corner of their house. This sand pit had a never ending supply of beach sand. Seriously, we never ran out! We would gather our metallic, (most likely lead-based painted) cars and trucks and build all sorts of roads through our cities villages, etc in Scott's sandbox.

One summer afternoon, Scott and I were very busy rummaging through his garage in search of a toy. We moved everything that was in our way. Suddenly, a long tall metal pole got loose and came crashing down, right on my head. I was stunned. We never knew if Mr. Murray just happened to walk into the garage just then or simply heard our screams, but I recalled him rushing over to me, picking me up and taking me home. As we were all in my kitchen, for whatever reason, I remember him very clearly saying something such as: 'it's a good sign that it's bleeding.' This comment did indeed make me feel better, because it was really bleeding. As was the norm at that time, we didn't go to the doctor, the hospital or the emergency room, just put some bandages on it and let it heal. It did heal and the only mark left on my head was one of watching out for future flying metal poles!

If we got bored, we would simply get on our tricycles, (eventually we moved up to bicycles) pretend to dash to a fire and be the saviors of our town. Or perhaps we would try to become the future comings of Evil Knievell. We would ride our bikes on the sidewalk and for some odd reason think it was 'cool' to pretend to crash and fall off the bike and land on someone's lawn. If you made it to the Garbowski's bushes it was a big deal!

They had this great driveway with a seemingly steep hill. Truth be told it probably had an incline of 5%, but hey, it sloped! Come on, we were just kids!

Scott moved on. Sadly, we lost touch.

Johnny was next, a year younger than Deb. Because I spent my time with the 'older' Murray's, Deb knew far more about Johnny. She recalled very fondly these memories.

The 'older' Murrays also included the Maternal Grandparents: Mrs. Herrscher (grey hair) and Mrs. Murray (snow white hair). We didn't recall if they actually lived there or not, but they seemed to be at the Murray home quite often and treated me like I was one of their own. When our Grandmother passed away in 1952, for whatever reason, at least for me, we three boys did not attend some of her services, I was only three and a half so I may not have gone to any. I believe Grandma was waked at her home in Corona, NY. Mrs. Herrscher watched the three of us, (Deb wasn't born yet) and I remembered Dick and Jerry telling me all sorts of weird stories all night long. A few years later, we shared in their family sadness when both Mrs. Herrscher and the elder Mrs. Murray passed away.

Perhaps no other event strengthened the relationship more than the night that Mr. Murray was rushed to the hospital.

We didn't know what was going on, all us kids knew was that the Murray kids were with us and we spent the night talking about their Dad, who suddenly became ill. He was sent to Nassau Hospital in Mineola. It's a local hospital which was the forbearer of the mega hospitals that have become quite common on Long Island today.

Perhaps he had been sick for a while; but we never knew. As kids remember, we were trained to be seen but not heard! And details such as illnesses were often not shared with the young. It was a 'good' news mentality and culture. Everyone lived a dream or so it seemed.

I seemed to recall Mr. Murray coming home with some sort of bag attached to him to help him go to the bathroom. The facts behind this were never detailed. For all I knew he had figured a way to avoid holding it in while waiting on line! Fortunately he did get better and we all remembered playing together those memorable evenings and afterwards.

The Murrays moved on away from Memory Lane but came back for Dad's Funeral. Mom was touched. During his services, special mention was made of the true bond that Dad and Alex had for each other for years. A lot of tears were shed.

When Mom passed, some nine years later, the Murrays, who by now were, like Mom, somewhat elderly could not make the trip. They did, however, send most sincere condolences, which were truly appreciated.

Every year, Mrs. Murray and I write each other a beautiful family Christmas update. Each giving each other the news of our own families. Someday, my goal is to visit. Unbeknown prior to me, but due to our walk, I learned that my siblings exchange the same greetings as well. For that I am glad. I still feel a strong bond towards the Murray Family and am sure that Mom and Dad would surely want it to remain that way.

The Murrays taught me Guidance. Reflecting on these memories we proceeded to march in unison next door....

A Godparent is chosen
To Love and to Care
To fulfill a great mission
To always be there!

THE GILLENS / THE LUEBBERS

I told the story:

One spring day in 1961, Dad and I were alone in the car, heading to pick up Dick from St. Mary's High School. We were about five miles from home and chatting in the car about the Maris vs. Mantle quest for Babe Ruth's Home Run Record. I was in the front passenger seat and Dad was obviously doing the driving. This was way before seat belts were invented, or if they were invented, they weren't installed in passenger cars. We wouldn't think we needed them anyway, because we had Dad's arm.

If ever he had to stop short, Dad's right arm would come from out of nowhere and be right there in front of your chest, holding you back if needed. We know now that that was a stretch, no pun intended. But it really seemed back then, that it would work.

Dad had incredible strength for a man of a 5'9" frame.

So much so that I would call him Samson. I would say to him, 'Was your Dad's name Sam and you are Sam's son?" Eh, he didn't laugh either! (Samson = Sam's son, what you still don't get it!)

So Dad and I were in the car, driving at a normal rate of speed. Simply said, Dad didn't drive fast. Suddenly, I saw him growing a bit tense as he looked in his rear view mirror. He grew more and more anxious and I asked him what was wrong. He told me that there was a cop following us very closely for a few miles and now he's right on our tail. Within an instant of his saying that, the police car put on its flashing lights and siren, causing Dad to pull over. He was a nervous wreck.

As the cop gets out and starts walking to our car, Dad starts fumbling through his wallet to get his license and registration. I am watching this in childhood awe. I am thinking: 'What's going on? Is this guy Broderick Crawford from Highway Patrol coming to arrest my Dad! Or, perhaps they are after me because I climbed the backstop at the Lots baseball field! Just keep our cool! Breathe slow, keep the cool.'

The cop looks into the now open window, he asks Dad for his license and registration, then breaks up laughing – 'Frankie, it's me, Jimmy Gillen.'

It took Dad sometime to get the joke!

Next door to the Murrays lived the Gillens. We didn't recall much about them, except that they were seemingly a much younger couple than

Mom and Dad. We didn't remember if they even had kids! The one thing we did recall was that Jimmy Gillen was a Nassau County Policeman who once almost made Dad lose his cookies...and mine too!

The Gillens must have done well financially; at least that was what we were told. We thought this because supposedly they moved to a much larger home in a more affluent town called Garden City a few miles away. We visited them once or twice afterwards, but for all intents and purposes, our family lost touch with them.

They sold their home to a young family with three boys and a girl, their name was the Luebbers.

Mr. Luebber was an enigma to us. We didn't really know him too much. Their oldest son was named Karl, about a year or two younger than me. He didn't seem to be really into sports, and was harder for me to get to know. His two younger brothers were named Chuck and Stan. Stan was a very good athlete as was their younger sister Sandra.

I remembered Sandra excelled at kickball, which would normally be played after dinner in front of their home, because they lived at the 'T' corner of Macrame and Memory Lane. It was sort of like our 'unofficial' street 'field.' We would play stickball, football, steal the flag, ringaleaveo, kick the can, punchball and 'I do so Declare' in that section of the block. Hide-go-seek, however, was normally played in front of our house. Maybe because of the many trees that lined the block by our home giving us an incredible amount of places to hide our small bodies behind the large tree trunks.

For the most part, however, I didn't really bond to the Luebber kids. It was different with their Mom, Mrs. Luebber. She was really a cool lady.

She was friendly to all the kids on the block and would talk to all of us. When I was a little older, she worked in a temporary placement agency and helped me get odd jobs during various school breaks. Yes they truly were what should be considered odd jobs.

One of them had me working eight hours a day for two weeks taking staples out of magazines. I would literally come to work every day and have this huge pile of binders full of magazines in front of me. I never knew what the purpose of this was, I was bored silly. I never knew why they simply didn't throw these magazines out! Were staples that expensive back then?

This became the very first job that I actually quit; I have not quit many since. I went back to Mrs. Luebber and she found me another job working at Purolator Courier, doing accounting work. These positions gave me valuable and most welcome spending money and also ironically got me started in logistics before I even knew it. I remembered meeting a co-worker there who was a Jehovah Witness. During both our lunch and coffee breaks he would tell me all sorts of stories about how he once was Catholic and became so, so happy once he converted. I hope he still is. That wasn't my thing.

Mrs. Luebber was perhaps the first person we knew who experienced the terrible throes of cancer. She discovered a lump on her leg. It was tested and determined to be malignant. Medicine and medical care then was surely not what it is now and sometime later, she sadly passed on. She was a really nice classy lady. We all missed her. Their home never seemed the same. Sadly, they eventually also moved on. We never knew whom they passed their Memory Lane torch to.

The Luebbers taught me Inspiration....we went next door.

Dick, Mom, Jerry and Ron on vacation e 1955

THE KOTOKOWSKIS become THE MCINTOSHES

We didn't really recall the people who lived next door. We thought they were named the Kotokowskis. But odds were it was an Irish name; remember that's the way it just had to be. Memory Lane Rules! Once the unknown Kotokowskis moved out, the McIntoshes moved in and became an instant hit, a really cool block family with the right formula-kids who played!

They played ball; they ran; they played games. They so added to our legacy and lore of having so many kids on the block. We once even had our own Olympics! The Memory Lane Olympics of 1960. Rome may have held the big one, but we all participated in ours!

The McIntoshes' father was a teacher in the local

school system. He would be home earlier than most dads and come outside and play with the kids. Their dad also had a brother who was a priest, who would come to visit and play stickball with the kids on our block. It was like our own made for TV movie! All we needed was Bing Crosby!

We did not recall too much about their Mom. I guess she was just Mrs. McIntoshe and frankly, none of us could even recall what she looked like. But we remembered Mr. McIntoshe, and his brother, ironically much more than we did their kids. I often wondered if they were the same McIntoshes famous for the apple of the same name. Both men's faces resembled an apple!

Childhood Wonders

Then again, I wondered about a lot of things that no one else wondered about! A good friend of mine, Ken, once said that I have the incredible ability to know more things that are truly unimportant, but which in the grand scheme, turn out to be fun. Perhaps this is what this recollection is all about!

I remembered going to Mom in the middle of the night

wondering how the world could end...how can there be
no beginning and no end. Mom would calmly tell me
it's a mystery and I shouldn't worry about it...that it is
like a circle...with no beginning and no end. Or I
would wonder how God decided to make our bodies.
What made him think that giving us five fingers and
five toes made sense? Why are some people smart,
others not; some good looking, others not; some athletic,
others not. Why are there people on the earth and
nowhere else? Why was I lucky to be born in a free
country like America and not somewhere else? Why
doesn't spaghetti stay on my fork? Who invented keys?
Do nuns go to the bathroom? How does the mind
work? Can you feel it? How does it work with the
soul? Why is there homework? What in the world does
the plot and theme of a book mean? And who really
cares. Why do baseball managers wear uniforms but not
football coaches? Why is a football so oddly shaped?
What's heaven like? Where is it? Where was I before I
was born? How does TV work? How does a plane stay
up in the air? Why can Jerry throw a ball better than
me? Which is worse – being deaf, blind or not being
able to taste something? Where do fingernails come
from? What made me think of these things?

The McIntoshes did not stay on our block for a
long time. For whatever reason, in a few years
they packed up and left the friendly confines of
our avenue and were replaced by a family none of
us could remember. So basically the McIntoshes
replaced a no name family and were then replaced
by another no name family. That's a bookend that
is certainly bland. Or perhaps it was simply our

lack of memory.

Major Sports from Memory Lane

While Mr. McIntoshe may have been a seasoned phys-
ed teacher, our block really didn't need one. We were
self coached, self managed and self contained. So much
so, that Alexander Murray, Kyle Gates and a few
others, being intrigued by what was going on in the
Rome Olympics in 1960, decided to organize our very
own major sporting event. Designed so all of our kids
could participate, it was fair, fun and festive. We
cornered off a section of the block which consisted of
some eight houses and held numerous events. Track
and field, baseball, softball, basketball, etc. What Rome
did, we did! We even had medal ceremonies staged in
front of the Gates' house! We called it: The 1960
Memory Lane Olympics!

Dad and two of his grandsons: Jim and Kevin, having a catch e 1986.

The McIntoshes taught me Sportsmanship and we
walked on.

THE GARBOWSKIS

THE CUNNINGHAMS

Ah, the house with the best sloping driveway on the block! A pinkie (Spaldeen) would probably have a problem running downhill on this slant, but to the kids of our street, the Garbowskis had The Indianapolis 500 for a driveway!

We used it to ride our tricycles, bicycles and roller skates. Not the kind that have evolved today, but the roller skates that actually had keys. Skates that were later popularized in a Maureen McGovern song called 'I've Got a Brand New Pair of Roller Skates and You've Got a Brand New Key.'

Roller Skates were cool, no one had skate boards back then, they were to become a craze that started in California and spread to the East years later. But anyone who had any sense of adventure would have a pair of roller skates that would be passed down through the family. The coolest thing was that they were adjustable. With that Special Key, one could open them up. With your shoes still on you simply slid your feet into this metal contraption. You had to wear shoes (Buster Brown's or Cowards?) because Sneakers (usually Keds or Nationals because Nike and Adidas were still visions in some marketing genius' cranium), didn't work as well with skates. So, you slid these babies on and suddenly, when you were on the Garbowski's driveway, you and your buddies became unofficial contestants in Roller Derby.

What's Roller Derby?

Glad you asked! Roller Derby was normally on late Saturday evenings on Channel Nine and featured people on roller skates who got their kicks going in circles, with a little bit of wall slamming hockey added to it to make it interesting as they strived to pass by their opponents. I always thought Jerry liked one of the women roller bladers; he seemed to watch them perform far more than the men teams. Of course this was always on just after Mom and Dad's mandatory Lawrence Welk Show on WABC Channel Seven, which featured Dick and Jerry's favorite act – The Lennon Sisters starring the young and beautiful Janet Lennon. (I knew he liked her since I once found her pictures in Jerry's drawer, so I had proof!)

The Garbowskis had a son who played with Scott Murray and me and we had a grand time, though I always thought he liked Scott better, (childhood issues come home to roost!) The family would do fun things, or so it always seemed. A favorite was when they would actually make their own ice cream for us. This was so cool! Really, that was a big thing. Maybe not as big as when our first color TV was delivered, but it was a big event!

I Scream, You Scream, We all Scream for Ice Cream!

No one else back then made their own ice cream! Getting an ice cream was a huge treat. The ultimate was going to Hildebrandt's, which was the all time best. Otherwise the Bungalow Bar, Good Humor or Mr. Softee trucks would come jingling down our street peddling their goodies. Everyone would yell: "Stop", hopeful that some parent would give in. Normally they wouldn't. On hot summer nights, we would occasionally go to the local Taystee Freez shop, which looked similar to Carvel. Their marketing must have had issues because they didn't survive the neighborhood and moved out of town. It sure wasn't the ice cream! After winning baseball games, our little league coaches would take us there to celebrate. I didn't recall too many visits, which could be a reflection on the quality of our play, or me as a teammate.

The only thing bigger than making ice cream and riding on their driveway was when both the

Garbowskis and the Murrays took a bunch of kids to the old Roosevelt Field, which later became an enclosed shopping mall. Roosevelt Field was the site of Charles Lindbergh's monumental first non-stop trans-Atlantic flight in 1927. He flew from New York to Paris. Besides being an airfield, the modern era took over the area and little by little made it into a huge two story shopping mall, becoming the largest of its kind in New York State.

The 'Bums'

One night, some players from the Brooklyn Dodgers were scheduled to come and meet the kids, sign autographs, and make us all feel very special. My memory of that early evening was my running around the open field playing with tons of kids, wearing our mitts and waiting. Waiting. Waiting! Until finally someone announced to all of us that the Dodgers couldn't make it. We never found out what happened; why they had a sudden change of plans. The next thing we knew was the Dodgers moved to Los Angeles. They were probably afraid of stepping foot back into our neighborhood! What a bunch of Bums!

Dad playing shuffleboard e 1946

Sadly, the Garbowskis and their son also moved away shortly afterwards. Happily, the driveway stayed. Gladly, the Cunninghams moved in!

Helen Cunningham became an endearing, loving trusted friend to Mom until the day Mom passed. They spent the day before Mom's earthly departure together, as they did many a Sunday, going to Mass and then to Friendly's for breakfast. Mom loved their Senior Special; you got a pretty good deal for a few dollars plus free coffee refills!

Helen's husband's name was Bob. We didn't know him too well; we did recall that he passed away at a relatively young age.

They brought four really intelligent children into the world. Their eldest, Bobby was quiet, quite musically inclined and very smart. Very smart. He played a mean piano and went onto a career in law as a DA. Their second, Janet, was one of the prettiest girls on the block and went onto become a physical therapist in private practice. Dan was the third and sadly, for the family, our block, their friends and especially his beloved Mom, his life ended tragically while in his 20's.

Their fourth was named Orin who truly became my personal favorite. We had a special bond. He was years younger than me, but was incredibly fascinated by the body cast that I had to wear during the summer of 1965 due to the spinal fusion operations I needed to correct my scoliosis. He would call me Turtle. This was years before Ninja Turtle, became popular. I proudly had that name first!

From Orins's perspective, I lived in my own shell. What a classic innocent way of picturing someone in a body cast, with arms, legs and a neck sticking out! He would hang around me all through the summer of 1965.

He was obviously year's younger but he was in incredible awe of this Teenage Turtle that lived and walked in his midst. Perhaps the rock group, The Turtles helped in creating the image as well! While I was tunefully challenged I could easily be, but couldn't sing 'Happy Together!'

Mrs. Cunningham became Helen to us. She was invited for family occasions that would celebrate many family events for Mom or Dad or for both of them. She would beautifully sing her Irish ballads at restaurants for us; her voice is as amazing as is her perspective on life. We could see why Mom and Helen both got along so well.

Though Mom was perhaps over 10 years her senior, they both had this youthful enthusiasm for life that carried them through life's hurdles. As time marched on, Helen's hearing grew weaker, but her passion for life, her wisdom and love for our family continued to grow. Helen has been gifted with an incredibly strong work ethic. She went to school and became a court reporter. Then, while in her seventies, she studied acting and joined the actors' guild, auditioned and landed small parts in the New York Theatre. A very cool lady! Simply said, she is a blessing that we most lovingly and gratefully share with her family.

While Orin was fascinated with my back, it would never have happened had it not been for a salesman from Robert Hall Clothing stores in the early 60's:

Robert Hall and My Back

Their jingle was played on the radio and television all the time. It went on and on about their great values and low, low prices. We listened, we sang and we shopped at Robert Hall, or we went across the street for really good bargains at John's Bargain Store, but I don't remember if they also had a jingle. Robert Hall had their cool jingle; I am humming it now!

It was Holy Thursday evening, March 26, 1964 when, after attending Last Supper services at St. Aidan's Church, Mom and Dad decided to take us to Robert Hall, a rather famous clothing store back them, so I could get a new suit for Easter. Surprisingly two things stood out about that. One: it's incredible that one could buy a suit on a Thursday, not to mention Holy Thursday, and have it back on Saturday, in time for Easter Sunday! Two, why was I getting a suit?

Looking back, I figured that I must have needed a new jacket for some occasion coming up, or Mom and Dad figured I was due to get my own new digs after having followed in the footsteps and clothing of my two older brothers! We had to wear a jacket and tie to High School and Jerry and Dick were for the most part both out of the house, in college and the Army respectively.

What followed that evening had the most profound impact on my life, with the only exceptions being marriage, parenthood and being a Papa.

As I stood on the block of wood for the salesman / tailor to measure me; he kept telling me to stand up straight. He repeated this to me over and over. Each time I replied that I was. He finally went over to my parents, concerned and said that there was something very wrong with me, something very odd, that was causing me not to stand up straight.

I looked at myself in the mirror, it seemed ok. Mom and Dad, who had seen me every day for my then 14 years, seemed confused. The salesman persisted. He showed them how my back was severely going to one side and my head and neck did not rest evenly on my shoulders. This went on and on for what seemed like an eternity. I just wanted to get out of there, away from this freak and get a jacket somewhere else. Mom and Dad finally promised the gentleman that they would indeed get me to a doctor and we bought the jacket, with a lot of alterations.

The following week, we went to our old family doctor,

whom Jerry affectionately always called, Dr. Painintheankle! His office was located in Dad's old town of Corona, and since he was the one who delivered all of Mom's babies, he was a most trusted family medical expert. The good doctor had me do all sorts of exercises for him, and found that while I may indeed have had an issue with my back, I also had something called spurs on the bottom of my feet which would cause pain and perhaps make me stand somewhat crooked.

This diagnosis did make some sense, since as a youngster I was often called 'pigeon toed,' my feet turned in, and to correct that I was told to pick up marbles with my toes. Fact: I can still do it, and my right foot is truly more agile than my left. Nice mental image, right!

My recollection was that Dr. Painintheankle wasn't too concerned about my back, (then again, Mom and Dad may have shielded me from any negative news as was the case back then), but he did suggest that we go to an orthopedic specialist to investigate it further.

Mom and Dad found a Dr. Grenzer who had done some work on someone they knew. I thought it was Dick. The doctor was local and a really cool guy. I enjoyed my visits with him. His initial request was for me to have a number of X-rays taken from all different angles. Fittingly, we had to go to a technician where Dad's insurance plan would be covered, but somehow the technician misread the prescription and instead of taking some six X-Rays they took about 30. While no

*one thought then that X-ray radiation was bad for you,
Dr. Grenzer was surely ticked. I, however, thought I
had a lot of cool pictures for an album.*

*During my examination, I remembered him having me
bend over to try and touch my toes and he would then
put pen marks all over my back. I was then told to
stand up straight. He called Mom and Dad in and
showed them the X-Rays. He pointed out areas on the
X-Rays that could have been cause for concern, but they
were fortunately ruled out. I remembered his exact
words, 'we are lucky it is this, otherwise we would all
be here crying.' He then showed my parents my back
with the pen marks and demonstrated how my spine
was becoming an 'S.'*

*The diagnosis was curvature of the spine, now
commonly called Scoliosis. While teenagers are now
tested routinely for this, it was relatively rare and
pretty unheard of back then.*

*We were told that the cause was idiopathic, meaning
unknown and basically it was predominantly found in
girls by a four to one margin.*

*My initial curvature was 57 degrees off. It was
measured by a combination of both the upper and lower
back. He wrote a prescription for a back brace which
had to be molded to my body. I was told to wear it all
the time, except when I went to bed. It was sort of like a
girdle with bars on the back and the sides. The cross
stitch on the front was to be tightened so as to try to
keep me straight. Jerry was the best at tightening this,*

but I hated it when he did it. He would make it so tight. He certainly made sure I couldn't escape!

The only problem was that I would escape and basically didn't listen to the doctor's advice. I would still play baseball, football, basketball etc. One summer day, we had this very important baseball game in which we were challenged by a bunch of kids from a neighboring block.

At that time, I was considered somewhat of a home run threat, and my presence was requested. I kept hemming and hawing about not playing, but my team persisted. The kids on our block didn't know of my condition, as the norm for the day was to keep family medical issues silent. I believe the only person who probably knew was Mrs. Burke, our next door neighbor and Mom's best friend and confidante.

I played the game without the brace, but when I got home, Mom and Dad found out and was I ever in deep trouble. So I would wear the brace more often. I also wore it to play my daily afternoon driveway wiffleball game with Adam Gates after school. Twice, while bending over for ground balls, I could hear and feel the brace break. Once, while playing stickball, I collided with another kid as he ran to first base. We both fell to the ground. Jerry almost blew my cover as he ran over to me, picked me up and said, in a somewhat loud voice: 'Is your back ok?' There were a lot of questions about my back from the other kids, which Jerry and I just shrugged off. We did, however, create somewhat of a buzz.

In high school, the principal and teachers knew and the only effect was I was excused from gym, which bugged me, because I really enjoyed it, especially when we played War or Bombardment. So instead of going to Gym, I was sent to the school library. Uh, really now! Not fun!

Throughout the course of that period, I misled Mom, Dad, my doctor and more importantly me, because I would not accept the fact that I had a problem and would still secretly remove the brace and play games with my friends. I was wrong, oh so wrong!

Around October of 1964, I went back to Dr. Grenzer for a checkup. He took a number of updated X-Rays, measured me and called Mom and Dad into the room. He told us that my curvature was progressing very rapidly and that we needed to see a higher level of specialist. Amazingly, I had gone from 57 degrees in April to 81 degrees off in October. The fact that I had no pain surprised him. I now regretted taking off the brace, but he didn't seem to think it mattered.

A few days later he called Mom and Dad and advised them that he had arranged for us to visit the St. Charles Hospital Scoliosis Clinic in Port Jefferson, about 55 miles from home. Little did I know that this would soon become my new temporary home and result in many life changing experiences.

Our first visit to the clinic was confusing and a bit dreadful. Even after an initial tour of the beautiful campus in which we saw the chapel, the large outside grounds, the coffee shop etc, I still didn't really get what was happening or perhaps refused to accept it.

I recalled our being brought into a hallway which was lined with nervous boys and girls and their parents. Someone called my name, and I was led into a small room by a nurse who gave me a blue hospital gown. She told me I needed to strip and to put this on. I had no idea where the open flap was supposed to be, the front? The back? Embarrassed as hell, I basically wrapped the entire darn thing around me, not realizing all the other kids were going through the same anguish.

I went back to the hallway and sat with Mom and Dad, a little bit breezier than when I left. We waited as one by one they would bring the other children into their individual meetings with some mysterious people.

My name was called and I was brought alone to the examining room, whereupon I faced about five doctors and nurses, who had all of my X-rays on the walls, and me now in front of them, sweating profusely. I could feel the droplets and was embarrassed. They had me do all sorts of bending, stretching, reaching, measuring, etc. They asked if I had pain. I said not really, except for some minor pain in the small of my back occasionally, which to me was not a big deal as I grew used to it. They let me go back to my parents and asked us to wait for a while, as they talked through my case alone. Mom, Dad and I were all called back in shortly thereafter and we were advised that I needed to have something called spinal fusion surgery and it had to be very soon. Within weeks!

I refused. I wasn't sick, I felt great and wanted to go back home, go to school and play with my friends. "An operation?" I said. "Are you kidding me?" I shouted passionately. I had no desire to get involved in this at all and emphatically told everyone there my intentions, or lack thereof... the doctors, nurses, Mom and Dad. I carried on for what seemed like a very long time. For whatever reason, they just let me vent. Finally, one of the doctors, Dr. Larry, asked if the two of us could go for a walk alone. He was a tough looking man, forceful, no bull, sort of like John Wayne in scrubs. You didn't want to say no to this man.

I agreed, at least I think I did, and the two of us went for what I thought would be a chat. We walked out the door, make a right and went to another hallway, down past a few doors until he opened one of them on the left. There in front of me was a room full of oddly shaped people, men and women whose bodies were twisted in all sorts of strange ways. It was devastatingly incredible. They were like human pretzels. It was one of the saddest sights that I had ever seen, these poor poor people.

Dr. Larry looked at me, and simply said, "Ron, do you see these people, they all had issues like you, but unfortunately they didn't take care of them and now we cannot correct them. However, we can fix you. And one more thing, just so you know, if you don't get operated on, besides the fact that you will certainly look like them, the real problem is, it will only be for a short time, because if we do not operate on you, you will not live past the age of 23."

I looked at Dr. Larry, looked again at these sad people and said: "When do we operate?"

During the course of the next few weeks, Mom and Dad downplayed the seriousness of the situation. I never asked what kind of operation I was to have. I never asked what the recuperation was. I had only been in the hospital once before, when I was five to remove my sick tonsils, and then I was given tons of ice cream as a reward. So I basically went about my business, told my friends I would be out of school for a 'short' while for a 'minor' operation. I had no clue as to what was to be my new life. Looking back, Mom and Dad knew their son well and this was indeed the best thing for me, as I never ever worried about what was to happen, which I surely would have if I had known.

From second grade to the beginning of sophomore year of high school, I had not missed a single day of school. Every year, I received the Perfect Attendance Award, and I strived to keep that going. But I now knew that would soon be over, little did I know, I would not return to school until my junior year. That was my biggest disappointment!

On the morning of December 2nd, 1964, Mom, Dad and Dick drove me to St. Charles Hospital to admit me. With the song, 'Charley Brown' ('walks in the class room cool and slow...') playing on the radio, I remembered that car ride very well. No one seemed upset, least of all me.

While Mom and Dad did all the paperwork, Dick went

and did something better; he flirted with the nurses, so much so that they all started to like me and kept asking about my older brother. While I had many dedicated nurses care for me throughout my time there, one particular nurse, Joy, was my trusted ally throughout my entire ordeal. Whenever Dick came to visit, I knew Joy would be my nurse, or so it seemed. She was phenomenal. The bond was strong, so strong, that when I was finally discharged, six months later, she came into work on her day off to bid me goodbye. I have never forgotten her yet never saw her again.

The floor I was sent to was an adult surgical floor, as opposed to pediatrics. The feeling was that since I was now fifteen, I should be with adults. (Boy, did I fool them!) It became a most interesting life-changing adventure shared with some 25 different roommates over six months.

My first room was with three young men, who were in their late teens and early twenties. Once Mom, Dad and Dick left, the fun began as the guys made the new kid feel welcome.

Frank was the cool guy, a Fonzy, who lived life dangerously. He was about to lose a leg because of a recent car accident. He was very happy to be alive. On his right and directly across from me was Steve, a very funny guy who would constantly keep us laughing with his funny stories, nurse pranks and never ending jokes. He was in for leg surgery, also due to a car accident. And to my left was Gary, Mr. Cool, who became the personal heart throb for one of the young pretty nurses, who always made sure to close the curtain when she attended to him. He didn't share what his ailment was, but we noticed that he certainly got a lot of 'closed door' attention.

Steve had a portable eight track player and he would blast the songs of the day, particularly Frankie Valli and the Four Seasons. To this day, whenever I hear their songs, especially 'Peanuts,' my mind slips right back to that room. Because of my new medical allies, I didn't have a chance to get homesick the first night. These guys were cool.

During the course of my initial time with them, I saw a different side of life. One time, Frankie's friends snuck in a bottle of liquor and he and his friends had a little private party, while one friend stood by the door as the lookout for the nurses. They smartly didn't share any with the new kid ...I was only 15.

The next day, my new beginning was to take place. I had no clue what to expect. The experience from the night before changed drastically. I was sent to a room for a cast, but I wasn't allowed to walk there, which drove me nuts, I had to go in a wheelchair. It would be the last time I would sit up, never mind stand up, for six months.

I was brought into a room which had a metal rack in the middle of the floor; sort of what you would think existed in the Spanish Inquisition. They removed my blasted hospital gown, meaning I was au natural and they laid me down on the cold rack, extended my arms as far as I could reach in a stretching motion, and then the good Dr. Kerner, whom I really grew very fond of as a friend, ally and trusted physician, proceeded to turn some clock like dial which stretched me out, basically trying to straighten my spine. When my body finally met the number they were looking for, they stopped and the nurses starting wrapping me in some felt like fabric. After that, I felt new warm and wet wraps placed on me. They were putting a body cast on me, from my chin to my pelvis. This was to set me straight prior to my operation which would be about three weeks away.

Dr. Kerner and I spoke throughout this process, he had a great sense of humor and knew I needed that, so he kept me distracted and laughing. At one time, he turned to me and said, "OK Ron, now you are supposed to ask me, 'Dr., can I play the piano when this is all done'? I say, certainly, and you say, 'Wow, that's great! because I can't play the piano now!"

I never learned how to play the piano, but I did learn to live with my cast even though there was a problem with my stomach. For whatever reason, I kept getting pains in my stomach and they couldn't relieve it. One day, Dr. Kerner appeared in my room with an electric saw and said we are going to fix the problem. He proceeded to cut a 12 inch circle in the stomach area of the cast, to let my stomach expand. Ahhhh, finally relief!

In the very beginning, once I got used to the cast, it was still a little like being on vacation. I had a great time with Frankie and the boys. Frankie now had his leg amputated and couldn't walk, but he could ride a wheelchair really well. Somehow he convinced the good nurses that he and I needed to go for a 'walk' and meet the other people on the floor. They agreed, got me on a stretcher and put one legged Frankie in his wheelchair. He proceeded to push me room to room to meet our neighbors. We had a blast!

It was during this 'walk' that I met two most interesting people. A young girl, my age from Seaford, NY who had the same problem as I did. Her main concern was that she loved to ride horses and they assured us both that after our operations, our backs would be stronger than ever, but we were not to ride horses ever again for fear of falling and doing damage. This devastated her and we spent countless hours on the phone. Besides my consoling her about her future without horses we would also compare notes on the steps we made on this shared medical journey. Ironically, once we finally were released from the hospital we lost touch, more coincidently, I did indeed find my one true love in her same home town, as my Chris comes from Seaford! You can't make this stuff up!

The other patient was a young fellow my age who was the victim of an accident. He was a handsome, blond young fifteen year old, who looked very fit and trim. His attitude was incredibly positive, but his problem blew me away. Due to his accident, he was paralyzed from the neck down, for life. He could only move his arms and head and that was it. Nothing else. We would talk about sports and school and life in general. He never complained. He was so amazingly positive.

I always admired his courage. He truly made me feel most thankful that I was only in for 'minor' surgery.

I was a fan favorite back home. I would get visitors from the family as often as possible. However, one person I really wanted to see was my little sister, but because she was only nine years old, she was not allowed to visit me. It would be months before I saw her again.

One Sunday, my cousins, Barbara, Marjorie and Eleanor came to visit me. They knew I loved the Mets, that's my team, always was and always will be. They signed my cast, but added something extra, which caused quite a stir a few weeks later. Barbara took out a heavy black marker and in big bold letters wrote, "Let's Go Mets" on my plaster armor.

It was mid afternoon, on a cold December day, not much going on in the hospital, as I lay in my cast embraced hospital bed when suddenly I heard a ruckus coming from the hallway. There was some sort of commotion going on and a lot of people were talking and making noise. We had no idea what was going on when suddenly Dick comes into my room surrounded by other members of the media, with flashing light bulbs on their cameras. What was going on?

Stepping through the crowd came one tall strapping figure. He approached me and said, 'Hi Ron, I heard you were a great Met fan and the Mets and I wanted to wish you good luck on your operation!'

I looked at him and said: 'WOW, You're Larry Bearnarth from the Mets! What are you doing here?' He went on to tell me that Dick asked him to come and cheer me up. Then he saw my body cast, with the big hole in the stomach with the words: "Lets Go Mets' emblazoned on my plaster belly. He gladly signed right next to it and said: 'Gee, you really are a big Met fan aren't you!'

We spoke for a while about the previous season, his appearance in the famous record breaking 23 inning game against the Giants, how he was injured for part of the year, and our mutual hope for the coming season.

All the while, the cameras were flashing and I felt like I was back in the newly opened Shea Stadium watching my beloved baseball warriors at play. It was phenomenal. A moment in time which I will never forget what my brother Dick did. How he pulled it off was beyond me, but obviously not beyond Dick. My picture appeared in the papers and I became sort of a local poster child. My Aunt Estelle carried the picture in her wallet always, until she finally gave it to me, but only after she ran into the one and only Jackie Robinson at a charity event and went up to him, told him about me, showed him the picture and had him autograph it for me.

But my most memorable autograph is the one from Larry Bearnarth, on my cast, who became my personal crusader. I followed his career throughout baseball and always cheered him on, no matter what team he played on or coached!

The following spring, while I was still lying in the hospital bed, the Mets started spring training. My Aunt Violet, Dad's baby sister, heard of my visit from Larry Bearnarth. She went to their training complex with an unsigned Get Well Card, tracked down my favorite pitcher, told him who she was and asked him if he would sign the card. Rather than simply sign it, he took it from her, passed it all through the club house, onto Casey Stengel, Yogi Berra, Warren Spahn and all of the Mets players who then signed their autographs for me. When this card came in the mail, it was overwhelming. Talk about brightening a kid's day!

My claim to fame spread through our village of Williston Park. On the rare occasions when I was allowed to come home from the hospital, in between operations, in a stretcher, the Fire Department would send their ambulance to drive me. One day, they came to the house, but I didn't think I was to go back to the hospital just yet. No they said, we have someone who wants to meet you. So they put me on the stretcher, and rode me to our village pool where the Mets All Star Second Baseman, who was on the disabled list after getting hit on a cheap shot by St. Louis Cardinal second baseman, Dal Maxvill, was making an appearance. The ambulance pulled up, they wheeled me out and Ron Hunt comes over to me to chat. It was incredible. He asked me how I was doing and said the team was thinking of me. I was floating on air!

My two favorite Mets – Larry Bearnarth and Ron Hunt! It couldn't get any better than this!

My Mets Get Well Card from 1965 Spring Training

Years later, the summer of '88, Chris and I and our three boys, (Chris was pregnant with Kaitlin at the time, so in essence she was there also), were in Montreal on vacation.

The Montreal Expos, now Washington Nationals were playing and we bought tickets to see them play. Larry Bearnarth was now their pitching coach. I called their front office, explained who I was and what Larry had done for me 24 years earlier. They were very touched by this and arranged for me to meet Larry. We were told to go to a special gate inside the stadium. All of a sudden this tall man in his now Expo's uniform appears. I told him that his hospital visit from years earlier had inspired me and I always wanted to say thank you to him. We chatted, he saw my three young boys, who were ten, eight and six and all wearing Mets apparel, and he asked if they wanted to visit the clubhouse. Visit the Clubhouse? Don't ask twice! WOW!

He mentioned that Chris, because she was a female was not allowed in, (this rule has since changed). The five of us entered and saw the Expo's team intact, getting ready for the game. It was awesome. Then Larry took a sack of baseballs, went over to the boys and said 'how about some baseballs kids!' He then signed a number of them for us all. One of which is enshrined on my office wall.

Larry Bearnarth has become a legend in our household. True, he didn't have the lifetime stats of a Tom Seaver or throw the ball as fast as a Nolan Ryan. But to me, he *embodied what sports are really meant to be. He cared enough to make me feel special when I really needed it. And then, 24 years later, when all I wanted to do was to thank him, he did it to me again!*

Larry Bearnarth and my boys 1988

Dick worked for ABC Radio News and WABC 77 Radio at the time and he got to know the Disc Jockeys

rather well, especially HOA – Herb Oscar Anderson, who would passionately make a plea to his morning show listeners to send a card to me while I was confined to my hospital bed. I would get cards and notes from so many people; we had to put them in boxes. I also received phone calls from various ABC announcers. John Cameron Swayze, of Timex fame – 'it's still ticking' - wished me good luck. It was totally awesome and took me away from what was about to happen in a matter of days.

The afternoon of December 20th, after being in the cast for three weeks, the good doctors came and cut it off of me. Mom and Dad were there and they gave them the cast to keep as a souvenir. Only someone like me would save it, which I did! They then told me I was going to receive a special whirlpool bath to sooth my body in advance of the operation. No doubt to also cleanse me after not having anything but delightful sponge baths for 20 days. I never knew if it truly was standard pre-op procedure or a special request from my roommates!

I remember being placed on a gurney, which was attached to my stretcher. The arms came down, picked me up as I lay there. It moved me directly over an iron tub full of warm moving water. Ahh! It felt wonderful. I then was hoisted up, placed back on the stretcher and sent back to my room, whereupon some nurses came and gave me an incredible back rub and then took out some razor blades and proceeded to shave my hairless back. This seemed strange, but who was I to question.

The next morning, nurses started coming into see me

early and proceeded to give me injections, for the pre-op I was told. Then the ambulatory crew came to get me, four of them picked me up, as I was not allowed to stand, and placed me onto the stretcher. The stretcher and me were like a team. Who needed a car or a bicycle when you had your own stretcher! We went down a few flights to a room that was shut tight by two large metal doors. Suddenly the doors swung open. I remember yelling out, 'Hey, this is just like Ben Casey!'

I was brought into the operating room, told everything would be all right and that I would wake up when it was all done. I was told to count backwards from 100. "99, 98, 97, 96"......"when are you going to operate I said." The surgery was done.

The four hour spinal surgery operation was over; I was in a recovery room fading in and out. As I was wheeled back to my room, I heard the nurses positioning themselves to place me back in my bed. While I know the nurses were truly careful; it certainly felt like I was swung on the count of one – two – three from the stretcher to my bed. It was excruciatingly painful. I let out a screeching yell from the pain. One of the doctors said, 'don't worry Ron, you will never remember this.' I did. I told him, 'Doctor I will never forget you saying that'...and I never have, but not much else.

I remember Mom and Dad coming into my room, and perhaps Dick and Jerry. I was heavily drugged. I looked at the bag of intravenous blood that was attached to my bed and slowly entering my body. I saw all sorts of family and friends faces in the bag. Mom thought I was freaking out. I kept saying things like: 'Look, there's Uncle John,' or 'Wow I see my friend Don Becker!' I bet Mom freaked out. I fell into a deep sleep.

I woke up four days later not knowing the day nor date. It turned out to be the morning of Christmas Day and as Dad parked the car Mom happily walked in to see me. I was in pain, ticked off and I proceeded to rip into her for putting me through this. It was horrible. I was mean and cruel. I am sure that she felt terrible. But she never ever brought it up to me, never. Never one word. It was a side of me that I certainly didn't like and I blamed it all on drugs. For that one single reason, when I later went onto college, which was during the Age of Aquarius with people tripping, smoking pot, hallucinating, experimenting, or whatever, I never partook in it. I knew firsthand what drugs could do to the mind and I never wanted to have it happen to me again.

During the course of the day, I calmed down and we 'celebrated' our family Christmas, again without Deb because she was still not allowed to visit, even on a major holiday! I received gifts, but for the first Christmas I could ever recall, I didn't give any. But my family was happy to see me smile, and from what I was told that became my Christmas gift for them.

Our celebration didn't last long as we were advised that I would need another operation in six weeks. The first one only did the upper and lower vertebrae and they would need to go back and do the middle ones. During the surgery, my back was split open, exposing my wavy spine; they then removed part of my right hip bone, made it into a jelly type solution and wove it in between my vertebrae. They saved the middle vertebrae for the second operation since it was felt that it would be too much to do it all at once. Great, I thought, we need to do this again!

Stitches I learned itch as they heal. I had two layers in my back, the deep ones would mysteriously go away on their own, and the larger staple ones, would have to be removed.

A few weeks later, they removed these, but the itching continued. At least the pain, helped by a combination of shots and pills, was easing. I would reach my hand behind my back and scratch the itch. I later learned this was not the right thing to do. Slowly my body was being infected, so slowly that it didn't show up on blood tests, until one morning when I awoke in a bed pool of blood. The staff rushed in, found out I had a seriously contagious staph infection and I was placed in isolation. Visiting hours were limited and even then only upon approval. My guests also had to wear special sterilized white gowns. One day, my Uncle Eddie, one of Dad's older brother's came to visit me by himself. He ignored the large signs, robes and warnings and crashed into my room. I was thrilled to see him and thought it was pretty funny how he did that, the hospital didn't.

As the infection faded away, I was sent home for a few weeks to heal and prepare for my second surgery, which would be on February 2nd. This was a treat. I was going back home! Even though it still meant I still had to remain lying down in bed, at least I was going home to the 'new bedroom' Mom and Dad converted from our living room with equipment obtained from the fire department. I really enjoyed those two weeks seeing my family, Deb, friends and neighbors as well as my tutors!

The night before my second operation my roommate, an odd duck who was a bit sarcastic and somewhat critical fellow in his thirties, started talking to me about life and his peculiar beliefs. With the room filled with both the background music of Petula Clark and her latest hit 'Downtown' or the playing of Nat King Cole's numerous songs because he was thought to be dying, we would talk about life, medicine and myths. I remembered his telling me how idiotic it was that health professionals published studies that actually said that eating too much bacon was not good for you. He would say, 'can you imagine this! 'They say bacon is not good for you? What's next, hot dogs?' Such was American dietary suggestions back in 1965.

This medical genius then went into what he had heard about my operation which was now a few hours away. He gave me his take on it: 'It's incredible; let me tell you, you are one brave kid letting those doctors cut you up like that! All you need is one little mistake by a doctor, a cough, a slip, whatever and you will be paralyzed for life! Good luck kid!'

I laid there listening to this and for the first time I had a little fear but told no one.

The second operation was successful, no infections and clearly the pain didn't seem as bad. Perhaps I was getting used to it or it wasn't as major. After all, they only did my middle vertebræ this time and used my left hip bone for the magic hardening solution. Guess I manufactured my own crazy glue!

I was sent back home to recuperate. Over the next few weeks, I would go back and forth to and from the hospital, via the fire department ambulance, for checkups, still laying down.

During this time, my St. Mary's Catholic High School arranged with our public school to send tutors to our house so that I could keep up with my studies.

I recalled having had three tutors – Math, Spanish and English. They were all very good, dedicated educators who passionately helped me stay on course with my class so I could graduate on time, even though I would be physically out of school for most of the year. To add to the fun, my Spanish teacher would bring his white poodle with him as well.

Upon my return to the hospital, a bed was hard to come by. The first night I had to stay in the hallway, oddly next to my former room which contained the bacon lover. It was dark and quiet and on my hallway night table were paper and a pen. In my best handwriting, I wrote in bold the word: ISOLATION and asked an orderly to tape it 'back' on the door, saying it had fallen down. He did. In the morning it was funny watching the staff do cartwheels trying to figure out what happened to 'Mr. Bacon' as they initially avoided entering his room!

Over the course of my time in the hospital, my number of roommates totaled 25. Many became distant memories. A few lasted. One was a minor league baseball player who was a teammate of Mickey Mantles!' I really truly enjoyed <u>his</u> detailed stories.

And then there was Hank White. Hank was a somewhat cantankerous gentleman of sixty five who was in for a routine operation. Hank didn't have much of a family and didn't really want to even talk to the nurses. For some odd reason, he would only talk to me. One day, as he lay in bed, I noticed strange gurgling sounds coming from him. It was frightening. I rang the nurse's button and yelled for help. They came running in and took him away. Days later he returned again to the bed next to me but now he could no longer speak. Hank had a stroke.

Hank continued his uncooperative ways with the nurses whenever they tried to care for him. It was painful for them as he would just ignore their requests. I started talking to him and tried to reason with him, me talking and Hank listening. He responded with his eyes. I became his ears and voice. In a weird sense, we could relate and the nurses started asking me the questions for Hank. I would ask Hank and he would visually respond to me. The nurses took note and tended to his care. I felt special that I was indeed helping my good friend Hank. Here I was fifteen and he was sixty-five but we had a special bond. When it came time for me to finally be discharged, we 'said' our goodbyes.

I called the hospital a few days later to speak to Hank, hoping someone would place the receiver next to his ear. As I asked to be connected to him, the operator simply said: 'Are you family?' knowing he had virtually none, I hesitated and said: 'Yes.' She then proceeded to tell me that unfortunately Mr. White passed away earlier that week. It was a most empty feeling. I hung up and said a silent prayer for him. I have never ever forgotten Hank White. He was a special, calm, gentle man. He reminded me in many ways of my Dad, who sadly ended up communicating in a very similar way.

My very best friend in the hospital was our chaplain, Father Moynihan. He would come to see me every day and we would talk about everything. We shared such wonderful stories. He knew I loved the Mets and we would talk about the games, the season, the players.

He was a wonderful older caring man who would surprisingly appear at just the right time, whenever I needed him, it was as if he had a supernatural sense of being. When my mind would go astray, he would bring it back.

I was suddenly 'discharged' on a June Sunday morning, while he was in church saying Mass. Sadly, while thrilled to go home, I didn't have a chance to say goodbye to my friend, Father Moynihan. Later that day, he came to visit me and saw my now empty bed. In the mail a few days later, came a very official looking

'Summons.' It seemed that I broke a true bond of friendship, he wrote, because I didn't tell him I was going home! The packet contained pages and pages of funny jokes. It was classic. That summer, Dad and I visited him at his retreat house. It was great. Two friends strongly separated by generations, but emphatically bound by a strong allegiance to each other.

Many years later, I had heard where he lived and went alone to visit him again. I was led to this quiet lonely room and out came a very elderly man who reminded me so much of my own Dad who had just succumbed to Alzheimer's. Fr. Moynihan was indeed there in bodily form, but mentally he had no idea who I was. It bummed me out. Dad and Father Moynihan! Why!

As Mom and I waited for Dad to get the car to drive us back home that memorable Sunday for my discharge from the hospital, Mom and I sat in the lobby; me in the mandatory wheelchair, which I couldn't wait to get out of and Mom next to me.

Since the back of my head was either in a cast or flattened down in bed for six months, I had grown very long hair at the nape of my neck. To say it was very long would be an understatement. It was also the early beginnings of a era when 'hippy type' characters were not really socially accepted. As we sat there, some older women happened to walk by, they made note of my long hair and uttered some comments under their breath. Mom heard this and ripped into them. It was classic.

As my back strengthened so did my view of life. For the

six months I was laid out on my back, I grew to appreciate the little things in life that one takes so much for granted. When we got home, my body again wrapped in a body cast from my neck to my pelvis, Mom asked me what I wanted to do. I replied, all I really wanted to do was to walk unaided to the kitchen sink and get my own glass of water, all by myself. For six months, everything was given to me and I wanted so much to do for myself. Reaching in the cabinet, grabbing the glass and drinking that single cup of water meant so much to me! Freedom!

By the way, the next day we went to the barbershop!

We would go back to St. Charles for checkups every few weeks. One particular visit, a whole bunch of doctors waited for me in the examining room. They appeared to look extremely serious and concerned as they reviewed my X-Rays. They talked amongst themselves in a low hum. Finally one of them turned to me and said in a low voice: "Ron, we have a problem. Your back didn't set right and we will need to do it all over again." I freaked out and started saying really intelligent statements such as "NO WAY!"; "I served my time"; "I'm not going back in there again!"; "Please, please, please.... get Dr. Larry!"

Somehow, someway, someone did manage to get my favorite surgeon, Dr. Larry, to come into the room. In what appeared to be his best John Wayne impersonation, he calmly strolled over to the wall with the X-Ray's, carefully examined them, stoically walked over to me and said, 'Ron, go home, everything, and I *mean everything, is perfectly ok. They simply misread them.' Anguish to joy within seconds! I loved that doctor.*

I was Orin's Turtle during the summer of '65

When our life returned to what may be considered a state of normalcy, Dad, who had a passion for letter writing, wrote a note of thanks to the Robert Hall Company, specifically thanking that special salesman who went out of his way to speak up, while others would remain quiet.

In Dad's words, this man saved his son's life.

About ten years after surgery, I developed a wound in my back that would come and go but would not leave me. I would go back and forth to the doctors to have it tested but no one could find out what was causing this mysterious opening. I had to bandage it all the time. Because of it being an open sore I could not go into any sort of swimming pool or the ocean for fear of an infection. I had to tape my back for showers, especially when I would travel to some third world countries. Some 20 years later, my youngest son Ryan, wanting his Dad to one day join him in the family pool, would pray incessantly for my back to 'heal.'

Months later, one morning while I was in the shower, I felt something sharp start to come out of the opening in my back. It felt like a very small piece of plastic. Angrily, I threw the dime size clear substance away. We now believe it was a piece of spinal disc that was logged in my back and could not be seen by an X-Ray. Amazingly, the wound soon healed and has stayed closed. I finally went back into the pool, for the first time in years with my family. Thanks Ryan! Faith can move mountains and also heal backs!

Prayer Works!
Me in my First Communion Outfit with Deb in the family playpen e 1955

The good doctors and nurses taught me respect for and the value of Education and properly using it.

Physical and Emotional Scars

For many years afterwards, I would not take my shirt off, anywhere, especially while at the beach. I was always embarrassed by my railroad track like stitches that stretch the length of my back from the nape of my neck to my tail bone. That was, however, until I met my wife. We spent many a day of our courtship at the beach, with her many friends. She made me feel incredibly comfortable and I would gradually forget the fact that I had these scars emblazoned on my body. It never mattered to her and thus I started to not let it affect me anymore either.

Nightmares & Dreams

As a kid, I would have two recurring nighttime occurrences. One good, one not so good.

First the not so good: The only nightmare I recalled was one where some sort of large rabbit would come from nowhere and start chasing me until I woke up. I would try to rationalize it, realizing how stupid a dream this was and eventually the rabbit stopped making his evening visits.

Now the good: For years, my dreams were pretty constant in one strong regard. It started at about the age of seven and I would be in many different exotic places. There would always be me and a beautiful blonde girl. This gorgeous gal was always in my dreams for many, many years. This was a time of true personal youthful innocence and my dreams surely met that mode. Sorry for the voyeurs in our midst but nothing wild and crazy happened in these dreams in any sort of erotic sense. However, imagine my sense of joy when the morning after my wedding, I awoke to discover that the beautiful blonde girl of my life long dreams was now my wife.

With all due respect to Don Quixote and his personal Impossible Dream, my dream really did come true!

The Cunninghams taught me Determination. We spent a long time talking about them, but we needed to keep walking and so we did, next door.......

My 'Dream Team'

Chris, Ron, Ryan, Jim, Kevin and Kaitlin

THE RENTERS

Next door to the Cunningham's was the quiet house. We never saw anyone ever come or go there. It was very strange, nary a name nor a face even when Trick or Treating. We didn't recall ever getting a treat, and no one recalled dare trying a trick! Who knew whom or what lurked beyond those doors?

That all changed years later, when Mom, during one of her many life lesson talks about a number of items from her past such as her childhood, the Bronx, our Memory Lane neighborhood, etc. casually mentioned to some of us about her friends in this house. We said to Mom: 'hold on here, please play back the tape, people actually live in that house and you know them?"

Mom confessed that she didn't know who owned the home but knew the people who rented it and talked fondly of them. Perhaps it was a figment of Mom's imagination, for we never saw anyone there, but Mom did...and who were we to question!

Mom's Life Lessons

Mom had worked for a local company called Great Products for many years doing general office work: paying bills, filing, record keeping, etc. She really enjoyed this job and only left it because of one reason: me.

When I was laid up during and after surgery, I spent six months in bed both at home and in the hospital. While home, someone needed to be with me.

So Mom quit her job and stayed home with me while I recuperated. Because I was not allowed out of bed, she became my 'wheels,' confidante, voice, listener and mentor. We shared a lot of stories and I learned a lot about Mom's youth, her parents, her Mom being raised in an orphanage in Ireland, her Dad, who was a delivery man for a coal company who passed away when Mom was only 15.....

I heard about her Mom, a landlady in the apartment house they lived in, who got an infection due to a pen that cut her finger and she ended up with serious blood poisoning in her arm. I listened to stories about Mom's family – she and her siblings being forced to separate for periods of time during the throes of the Great Depression.   Estelle and Mom were sent to their Aunt's home in Massachusetts because our Grandmother could not afford to tend to them and their brothers.

I heard of her endearing love for her two brothers John and James, who in addition to Dad were her true heroes, (there were really three brothers, but the eldest died at the age of five before Mom was born). Mom read me the letters that she kept in her secret box that came from her brother John giving 'fatherly' advice to his young sister. She told me of her loving but strong competition with Estelle, who was always the baby of the family.

She relayed stories of going to the local candy store in the Bronx with her sister Estelle and their friends Amy and Carolyn Herrscher;   of her early boyfriends; of Estelle's boyfriends; of Estelle's poetry skills;   of her courtship with Dad, how they met in Lowes Theatre in Queens, Dad the general fix it man who also put up the bright marquis and Mom the usherette who led people to their seats via her beaming flashlight. She went into detail as to how Dad would travel from Corona to the Bronx to be with her on their off days; how Dad would take in her brother and sister when her Mom died because they had nowhere to live; how Dad was so devoted to his own Mother; how she never met Dad's Father (Pop) who passed away two years before they had met; of the hopes, prayers and plans she had for the four of us, that our lives would be much better than what she had. That was a big one.

She would read her prayers, her novenas – Mom had a novena for every occasion and would spend hours praying them. I remembered her nine hour novena which was used a lot; her St. Jude Novena – the patron of lost causes; we must have had a lot of 'lost causes' because Mom prayed to him a lot! Mom spoke of her church groups: her Rosary Society, her Catholic Daughters of America, and her Legion of Mary.

She talked of how she thought I could be the next Bob Hope – Mom loved Bob Hope and whenever he was on TV, it was a Must See Show, no taping or DVR back then – you saw it real time or didn't see it at all; she thought I had a great sense of humor and really loved it when I would kid around and joke with her. When Mom got going she had an infectious laugh. I would make Mom the butt of many jokes and she really enjoyed the banter, she would then give it right back to me. I called her our family's Howard Cosell, because she would 'tell it like it is!'

She proudly boasted about her Irish roots, of which she was most proud. It is an absolute shame that she never saw Jerry succeed in his quest to become a legalized Irish citizen a short time after her death; she would have been so thrilled....as would have Dad!

Finally, we talked a lot about the Mets, my Mets and Mom's Mets. She really enjoyed watching the games and was a most avid fan, so much so that we always enjoyed kidding her when they would show an instant replay of a homerun. She never quite got the instant replay concept and always said: 'Wow, they hit another one!

Mom and her boys: Dick, Jerry and Ron while on vacation

e 1955

Ironically, our last 'real' conversation was the evening before she passed away. It was a Sunday and my family had just returned from Shea Stadium after seeing the Mets final regular season home game of the year. They were heading to the playoffs for another year and Mom was thrilled. Mom was so impressed about a play that left fielder Benny Agbayani made to help the Mets *defeat the Expos 3 - 2. She went on and on with overwhelming excitement about Benny and the Mets. Weeks after her passing, I wrote a note to Benny advising him of the last joy he gave her. He kindly sent me a nice note back. Classy guy that Benny Agbayani!*

The Renters taught me Nothing, except that I learned to never underestimate Mom's ability to turn strangers into friends.....and we marched to the corner house....

From Dad's Wallet
There are also three girls and two more boys

THE BRETTS

Not too many blocks have homes that are distinguished by their animals, yet we had two. You already met the Weber's human like dog Gracie and next we visited the home of the largest dog on our block, Jake.

Jake was a huge French Poodle. We mean HUGE. This dog must have been a hybrid or perhaps it was fathered by Arabian / French horses. Black as the night with that curly French Poodle hair, everyone knew Jake and his home. However, no one really knew the Bretts except for Mom and Dick. Perhaps they were Irish, which would explain Mom's history with them. However, with regards to Dick, they must have had a daughter!

For the record, they weren't the same family as the

famous George Brett – from baseball fame, heck we didn't even know their first names!

Besides the fact that they actually didn't live on our block, they were the corner house and it faced Koch (actually called Koch Boulevard for the purists, but we would just use first names for most of the neighborhood streets). We did make an exception and added them to our 'block' because of Jake and two special things about their home.

1: They had a real pond on their front lawn. It was so cool, an actual small pond with real water. No one had these things, not on our block, but Jake did! We talked about the story that was old but still funny today…. Dick once fell into their pond.

2: They also had an old red tractor always sitting next to their pond. As kids we thought it was meant to serve a useful purpose, but the older we got we realized its purpose was simple > lawn decoration. The darn thing never moved off that spot!

Not much else was known or shared about the Bretts, but we did talk a lot about Jake, the pond and the red tractor, which was still there!

The Times, Trials and Tribulations of Koch Korner:

Dad worked a customary five day work week, but it was somewhat different than the norm. His always included four weekdays and Sunday; except for every seventh Sunday when he had it off. On the Sunday afternoons that he worked, just prior to our traditional family 'sit down dinner,' I remembered waiting for him at the corner of Memory and Koch so he could 'drive me home' from work. I would stand their anxiously looking down (or up) Koch in anticipation of his car coming from the busy Hillside Avenue. I felt so cool sharing the last leg of Dad's work journey with him.

I also remembered a time, while waiting for Dad that Jerry joined me. Along the way, he picked up some animal from the street and brought it home. He was thrilled. It was also a very dead animal, it was a dead squirrel! Mom wasn't as thrilled as Jerry.

On the corner, Dick also told us about his visit to his childhood friend Johnny Antioselli, who at nine thought he was a skilled apprentice carpenter and builder of very sharp contraptions. He tried to build a hatchet to chop through wood in his basement. One day, with Dick at his side, he did a show and tell for Dick's benefit. Unfortunately it came down too quickly and chopped off his thumb...it really did. And this was before medical science perfected the art of reattaching 'detached digits' to a hand! Poor stupid Johnny. Dick claimed they found Johnny's dumb thumb the next day on their basement floor. Good thing it wasn't his toe, or they would have had to call for a tow truck! (I just had to write that!)

Finally, my lasting memory of the Brett's corner was a day that I really lost my temper with Mom and Dad over something typically kid like stupid and I said some really cruel things that caused me to run away from home. Up the block I ran. I was fast back then, at least I thought I was. This was years before my operations. I must repeat, I was a really fast runner. After all, I ran track. Hey, I even won a few medals. But I was a little mistaken about my abilities and my competition in this race. I totally underestimated Dad. I never knew that Dad was also fast until I galloped away and neared the corner by the Brett's house, when suddenly I felt two large hands pick me up by the collar, dangle me in the air and quickly end my run bringing me back home. Ah, sweet memories of Brett's Corner! Sorry Dad!

The Bretts taught me Creativity and we crossed the street....

Grandma, Aunt Mary, Uncle Bill, Mom and Dad e 1942

THE COOKS

THE CARUSOS

Our journey led us across the street to 'our' side! Our side was the south side of the street, not the sunny south side, unless you were in the expansive (expensive?) backyards on our block of 40′ by 100′ property lots. All kidding aside, all the kids on our block thought all of our families had a large amount of property. Actually, it was enough for a small patio, a garden, perhaps a swing, a driveway, a garage and a tremendous amount of valued memories.

Some houses however, were lucky enough to have the sun shine on the front of their homes but it surely wasn't us, our side got the north side effect and with it a massive amount of our neighbors leaves and snow! Being a lifelong snow shoveler, not by choice mind you, I firmly admit: it stunk!

Life lesson # 1: 'Always buy a house on the north side of the block!'

The Cooks lived in a big house, a large colonial that, along with the Jones's next door, really didn't fit in on our block. They were kind of fancy, rich looking homes. They must have paid more than the $10,500 Mom and Dad paid for our home in 1952…perhaps they laid out $12,000!

Except for playing touch football and stickball in front of their home, I only remembered one particular football game on a Thanksgiving Day playing with Dick, Jerry and the kids on the block before dinner.

Two things odd about this memory: 1: Due to wide age differences I do not recall playing together with Dick and Jerry often and 2: oddly, nothing stupendous happened in that game, but I actually did recall all of us playing it together and wondering why we were allowed to play on Thanksgiving Day! After all, that was like a Sunday clothes day! Everyone, except for the turkey lucked out.

We didn't really know much about the Cooks. They really kept to themselves. That is except for the day when we were playing a street ball game and an ambulance came screeching to their house.

We never knew why or for whom, but it was a scary scene and it stopped the game, which was quite a hard thing to ever do on our block!

And then there was trick or treating......

Memory Lane Halloween

Halloween was a block affair, at times scary, especially at night, if you were granted parental permission to trick or treat in the evenings. One had to avoid getting pelted with eggs and sock sacks filled with flour from the bullies who lived on other streets. The kids on our block surely didn't do that stuff! We would trick or treat in packs, most of us in our homemade costumes, except for the rich kids, who got to go to Woolworths or perhaps The Big D and buy that cardboard box, with the clear plastic cover that showed the latest Superman, Batman or Casper the Friendly Ghost Costume.

Somehow, someway, one year, I was fortunate enough to either inherit or acquire a Mighty Mouse costume. I absolutely loved that cartoon show, watching Mighty Mouse forever come to 'Save the Day.' I remembered once arguing with my friend, cousin and next door neighbor Scott Gates that when I put the whole costume on, I knew I actually could fly, but, as I would always tell Scott 'I decided not to' for fear of getting in trouble with the 'higher authorities' meaning our parents.

We talked about and remembered eating the treats as we tricked, and when we got home, for some reason, my loot was never as much as Dick or Jerry's. This always annoyed me! Why were they so much better at getting treats than me!

We also lived through the big scare of some sicko putting pins into kids' candy. This resulted in everyone having to undergo mandatory parental candy checks at home when we returned with the booty. Our parents would carefully feel through the candy for the suspected pins. No one on our block ever found one, but it made us all especially very fearful of the bags that were homemade!

Jerry's Pin

The only pin that I recalled that put fear into our lives was the one that occurred one morning as we were all getting ready for grammar school. Jerry came down into our kitchen and said he just swallowed a pin. Though for years he has vehemently denied this ever occurred, Dick and I recalled it vividly. What we didn't recall however, was his advising us of what it felt like when it came out the other end!

I always wondered – was it a 'safety' pin or straight pin? Ouch!

The Cooks moved on and were replaced by the Carusos. We really didn't know them too well, except for Mom and Dad's relationship through the Murray's. Mr. Caruso joined the local fire department; years after Dad retired from the force when he then became an Exempt member. The memory about the Caruso's that we did recall was that his brother was actually a famous sportswriter for a major newspaper, and he would sometimes be the official scorer at Mets / Yankee games. We felt cool with this, but little did we know what would happen years later with our own family in this sports journalism regard with one of my sons.

Dad dressed in his Sunday Suit e 1950

The Cooks and Carusos taught me Neatness. Both kept their home that way always. And walk we did to the corner of Macrame and Memory...

THE ELDERLEINS

Ah, memories of balls on grass and hedges trimmed so neatly they framed a beautifully landscaped lawn. It could only have meant that we were approaching the House of the Elderleins! But, aghast! The infamous blasted hedges! They were gone!

It is amazing how images can become reality but in oh so many ways are really quite unfair. On the corner of Macrame Place and Memory Lane resided the Elderleins. A home where the danger of trying to recover a ball that would land on their lawn was akin to trying to rescue Christians from hungry Roman lions! It was a fate most of the kids on our block dreaded, few dared and far less succeeded. If you failed, Mr. Elderlein would come out and yell at you! Really yell at you! Fear can cause strange emotions. The dreaded runs being one of them!

With so many kids on the block and with their lawn being manicured to perfection, one can understand the concerns of having young armies marching across the field of Macrame.

The Elderleins had three children, a son Cary, who was near Dick's age, a daughter Paige, around Jerry's age and a daughter named Cara, who was, for quite a while, Deb's best friend. As such, over the years, but in truly different eras, Dick and Deb spent a considerable amount of time in the Elderlein's home, as did Mom who became friends with their Mom, Cara. I only stepped in their hallway bringing Deb back for dinner. I never ever ventured further.

Cary was an enigma to many of us younger kids. He appeared bigger than others and seemed to know ingenious methods of how to get into mischief. Age has a lot to do with perspective!

We recalled two stories about Cary, one was when Dick had Cary and friends over to make jelly apples in our house and the kitchen became a caramelized mess. We didn't recall whose idea it was but history would probably prove that Mom walked into the scene in total shock at what her eyes beheld before her. I remembered seeing the aftereffects. It was not pretty. Eddie Haskell couldn't have done it better!

The second event was when Dick and Cary were doing another sort of prank in our house, and just before Mom and Dad came home, in the true spirit of the Little Rascals, Jerry and I recalled seeing Cary jump out of our kitchen window, running off to safety two doors away! The sight of him jumping out the window and running away still lingers! He was so quick! One wondered how a father so strict could raise a child so fearless.

Paige I didn't really know, though, she was most likely a part of Dick's inner circle. Cara was the quick witted funny child. Whenever she came over to play with Deb, she would have us in hilarious laughter over the things she would say. She was never at a loss for words. I remembered a game where we would all sit around, Mom, Dad, Estelle, Deb, etc. and I would quiz Cara as if she were a contestant on the Art Linkletter "Kid's Say the Darndest Things" segments on his TV shows of the 50' and 60's. She would come up with some of the most unusual and bizarre answers. She looked a little bit like a young Carol Burnett and shared a very similar sense of humor. A very cute child indeed.

Mr. Elderlein was an accomplished pilot, who went onto to train new pilots. I believe this promotion caused them to move away. Sadly a heart attack ended his career and his life. But Mom stayed in touch with their Mom, Deb stayed in touch with Cara, no one really knew what became of Cary, Paige or the new owners or who they were. To us, it was always the Elderlein's house, so much so that even on the day of our 'walk,' we didn't think of taking a walk on their grass!

Deb:
Daddy's Little Girl

Deb was the only one of us to have been born and raised on our block. Dick, Jerry and I all were all born in Queens. So Deb was really known by all of our neighbors as a true product of the block. After having three boys, Mom and Dad, our family, friends and our neighborhood were all so thrilled to finally have a girl in the family.

For years, I remembered Mom would refer to me as 'her baby,' which, when you are six years old, grows weak quickly, not to mention embarrassing. So I was quite happy when Deb came along to take over my infant mantle.

However the celebration about finally having a girl made me ponder what the reaction must have been by family and friends when the news of my own birth was announced. Probably something like, 'Oh, another boy, oh yeah, that's, uh, really great! That's, uh, nice. Good work Frank and Loretta, and when you are done can you pass the beans please…..hmmmm! (Ouch! I sense one of Mom's looks coming through the heavens now heading straight for me!)

When Mom was pregnant with Deb, we would all try to figure out names, yeah, as if we were truly part of the selection process! Dick was infatuated with Bridget Bardot. Mind you, Dick was a very healthy 13 year old who had a vivid imagination and pretty girls always fascinated him. He wanted to name his baby sister BB – Bridget Baumbach!

The movement didn't gather too much steam, but yearn he did to get a Bridget in the family. After Dick's long labor, as well as Mom's, we were finally told that Dad would decide the new baby's name. Supposedly, Mom chose all three of us boys' names. Why I was called Frank Ronald for three days, only to find it was too confusing to have two Franks in the house always intrigued me. Socially, I am forever Ron, with the exception of the first few days of my life. Legally, however, I am Frank. Now, years after Dad's death, I am most proud that he shared his name with me. I just wish we could have shared it together.

We never heard what Deb's name would have been had she been a boy, and surely in the '50's a baby's sex was not uncovered until birth. We only knew that Dad wanted to be creative and it was to be his final call. He had always liked the name Deb and thought of the uniqueness of naming his new daughter Debra Eileen Baumbach with her initials clearly spelling her name:

DEB. Classic move by Dad!

Upon Deb's birth and her arrival into our home, Mom recalled how she and Estelle were raised in a man's world and she pledged that her daughter would have opportunities that she didn't. This is not to say that Mom was a women's lib type person, in fact that movement was still years away from being a reality. But she wanted it known that Deb would be her own person, make her own decisions and never ever be a servant to anyone.

I would always play on this with Mom and pushed it to the nth degree. I had a knack for getting her gander going. When we were little, I would kid that Deb got to have butter on her toast, while I had to use margarine on mine or why wasn't I allowed to climb trees while my baby sister was. They were running lines that I had with Mom to get her Irish up, and it worked, especially when I was laid up for months in a hospital bed! Hey Dick and Jerry probably got Marmalade or Apple Butter and me – margarine! Mommmmmm!

Most likely due to the fact that Deb grew up with three older brothers, she could handle herself pretty well. She was also an exceptional athlete. Unfortunately girls' sports were not a major item back then; truly a loss for all sports. She would catch and throw a ball with me and would not miss my fastest hurls! Fact is Mom had a pretty strong arm as well! Genetics!

Rather than do what female athletes do now and play softball, basketball, etc, Deb took to baton twirling, Irish

Dancing and the 4H club. Since Dick and Jerry had already moved out, I would 'cheerfully' go to her various events and watch her perform, payback for her going to all of our games years earlier!

From watching far too many cowboy shows, I had a stupid trick that I would do with Deb quite often. It was masterful, at least to me. Just like in the movies, I would pretend to hit her with a quickly thrown fist, and as I would always just miss her, I would quickly slap my hand so it sounded realistic. (I saw that trick in some old cowboy and Indian movies). I had it down to a science, except for just one single time, when something went wrong. Maybe Deb moved, or my timing was off, but I hit her good. This time the sound was real! Dad and Mom were not too happy and I have never stopped apologizing for that act to my sister. That time became the last time we, or should I say, 'I' tried that trick. In a moment when we once again recreated television magic, I actually did 'lovingly' throw a pie in her face, which she took good naturedly. In fact, I think it may have been her favorite flavor!

Our home would be a haven for Deb to bring her various friends to our house from both the neighborhood and school. A home full of baseballs, basketballs, footballs, toy soldiers and box cars evolved to dolls, doll houses, makeup, art work and lots of chit chat!

Deb is truly her own person, possessing many of Mom and Dad's strong traits. Fiercely loyal, lovingly dedicated to her family and possessing a firm moral fiber, one sees so much of Mom in her. But truly, Deb was Dad's little darling, as most daughters are to their fathers. I cannot recall one moment when he was upset with her. She is forever their baby!

Deb and Dad - Always Daddy's Little Girl

We then took the 35 steps across Macrame, looked down the block, remembered those who lived there...the gentleman near the end of the block who was killed in a major airplane crash in the late 50's; the fellow who drove Mom back and forth to work every day to her tax office job for years; the young girl named Karen whom I always thought was cute but I was too shy to tell her; the gal next door to her with all those freckles, her brother who was a dwarf; the family who lived in between her and the Elderleins with their oh so many kids; our back door neighbors, the Jenkins who had a cool driveway with a fantastic built in patio in their backyard and a Annette Funicello looking daughter who drove the coolest blue convertible – always with the roof down, and of course there were the Dennehys.

Neighborhood Fame

A few houses away from us on Macrame lived the Dennehys. A very nice Irish family. The father drove a really cool station wagon, which I was always impressed with since it actually had wooden designs on the outside door panels. The family had three children, one of whom became an actor. I mean a real actor.

Our neighborhood celebrity was Brian Dennehy. Brian was a local college football star, and went onto quite an accomplished career on the stage and screen as a winner of the Golden Globe Award, two Tony Awards, the Laurence Olivier Award and multiple Emmy nominations for TV shows.

We remembered first seeing Brian as one of the original Maytag Repairmen on TV and thinking that was so cool. We watched with pride as his career would skyrocket into fame. My personal favorites are Cocoon and his portrayal of Willy Lohman in Broadway's Death of a Salesman for which he won the Tony as Best Actor.

Brian also gave back and I personally received the benefit of his giving. During my early teen years, just before my back surgery, I joined a local acting guild in our parish and Brian was our acting coach. Our production was Oklahoma and I proudly played the difficult and awe inspiring role of 'boy on stage.' I was quite pleased to be given a speaking part and had my one line dutifully memorized: "Here's a baby boy for you Miss Ellie, here's twins!" I never forgot my line! And I never forgot Monday evenings in the fall of 1963 practicing under the tutelage of Brian.

Over the course of time in the neighborhood Brian's parents passed away, and I remembered Mom going to their wakes and funerals. Brian may not remember the skinny 13 year old who kept trying to memorize his one and only line, but I am certain he would remember our Mom!

The Elderleins taught me Craftiness, after all, I couldn't afford to lose too many balls so I had to figure a way!   Brian Dennehy taught me the value of public speaking, for which I am indebted.

A 'family' gathering at our home with the Burkes and Gates e 1985

THE BURKES
THE MCNEILS

In life we meet all kinds of people, some stay with us for a short while, others a bit longer. It is sort of like a really long train ride. Some stay on for short trips, others for a much longer portion of the journey. You may choose to ignore, chat or start a lifelong friendship. You may meet them while in school, on the job, in church or in your neighborhood. Some simply go away while others make their mark and become a part of your very being and grow into family. The Burkes, as well as their in-law's the Ryans in essence grew into our family and us into theirs.

Our side doors were no more than 10 feet apart across a really tiny shared alleyway. Neither one of our homes had door bells on the side door.

For years, it was a very simple, <u>knock knock</u> – 'Mary, you home?' or, <u>knock knock</u>, 'Sister (meaning Loretta), you there?' And then each one would enter the home of the other, without waiting for an answer. If the door wasn't locked, it meant come on in! Frankly, this never felt strange. It wasn't an intrusion, and surely never an invasion of privacy. Both were as welcome as actual sisters growing up in the same home and going from each others' bedroom as they went back and forth this way for years.

When Mom and Dad married, they moved to Elmhurst, a small section of Queens in New York City. Their very first neighbor was a Mr. and Mrs. Ryan, who had three sons – Jack, Jim, Benny and a daughter named Mary.

Through this early sense of neighboring, an incredible attachment developed that lasted for close to 60 years. Mom and Dad and their then two toddlers and one baby (me), grew close with the elder Ryan's. It was so close, for us Mrs. Ryan wasn't Mrs. Ryan, she was always Grandma Ryan and it stayed that way until her passing away years later while in her mid 90's.

Once I was born, and everyone got over the fact that there were now three Baumbach boys, Mom and Dad realized they needed to get a larger space and started looking for their own house. They eventually bought one and moved us all to

Memory Lane in Williston Park. And who was their next door neighbor? None other than Grandma Ryan's daughter Mary and her husband Bob and their three sons – Bobby, Paul and Dennis.

A few years later, after Mr. Ryan passed away, along came Grandma Ryan who moved into the Burke home as well....so the circle of life came completely around!

Bobby and Dick were very close in age and the closeness grew in more ways than one. They became fast friends, sharing many, many memories, even though they were one year apart in school. They had a bond that many kids thought they might have had but the difference here was, for Dick and Bobby, it was real.

Sadly, I will never forget the following scene; it is forever carved in my mind:

Bobby

It was March 17, 1965, I was laying in the hospital bed that Mom and Dad set up for me in our once 'porch' which Dad converted years earlier to make our living room larger. I was home recovering from my two spinal fusion operations and waiting to go back to St. Charles Hospital in a few months to re-learn how to walk. It would be six months since I last took my own steps. Phones were scarce back then. Families had one in the kitchen, usually on the wall, and another, perhaps a fancy new Princess phone, in the master bedroom. Being I was convalescing, it was felt that a phone placed next to me would be a good idea in order to have me stay connected to the world. Cell phones didn't exist. No one heard of the internet.

It was around 2:00 P.M. when the land line phone rang. Reaching for it, I 'beat' Mom to the phone by a split second. As I was about to say 'Hello' I heard Mom's voice saying the same thing. There was no 'Caller ID, so you actually had to let the person talk to discover who was calling. I vividly remember Mrs. Burke screaming into the phone – 'Bobby's Dead, Bobby's Dead! It was frightening, her screaming shrills were full of so much Motherly emotion. I held the phone tight to my chest, never saying I was listening in on this, therefore I couldn't hang up. If not for their screaming, they would have certainly heard my heart beat. I never told Mom I was on this call. I could hear every terrible word. Mrs. Burke started to tell Mom what happened to Bobby. But the call wasn't long as Mom would quickly run into me, tell me with river flowing tearful eyes what had happened. She said that she would quickly go next door, if I needed her; I was to ask Deb, who was home as well. I knew she had to go to see Mrs. Burke.

Bobby was driving a borrowed sports car, along with one of his college friends, who, ironically was also named Bobby Burke. It was a very snowy day and the roads were treacherous, suddenly a truck was heading straight at them, he swerved but could not avoid the *impact. From what we had heard, the other Bobby Burke got out of his passenger seat, and only had a bruised knee. Our Bobby Burke lived a very short time before succumbing to his injuries. His school set up a scholarship in his name, and a local pub which he would visit when home, placed a trophy that his team won on display in his memory.*

I understood that while Mom was next door with Mrs. Burke, she held her, cried with her and mourned with her.

This was probably the only time during my illness that I was left alone without an adult in the house...but Mom was only ten feet away, Deb was there and I had a phone....that phone, I wished I had never picked up that call. More importantly, I wished the call never happened.

I cried.

Tragically, this was the truly the worst memory of our childhood.

The second scariest moment for me was the night of the First Big Black Out, the Big One, on November 9, 1965. Dick was home from his Army basic training and sometime during the evening, Dad had chest pains. We called our family doctor, Dr. Siegel and he made a house call, which is uncalled of anymore. Dr. Siegel liked Dad and the feeling was mutual, but I am sure that was not why he came, he came because of his calling.

We were all worried. What was wrong with Dad?
Was he going to die?

The word came out from the good doctor that Dad was
okay. I never knew what it was or what caused it or
what was given to relieve him, but Dad did get better.
For a few hours intertwined around the mysterious
Blackout, there was the larger fear of losing Dad.

The third scariest memory was the night when Mr.
Murray was rushed to the hospital for emergency
surgery. All their kids stayed at our house. I never
knew what was wrong, but I recall a great deal of
concern for his life....he may have had aftereffects but
survived the experience well.

Due to my having to stay in bed due to my
surgeries and not being allowed to be home alone,
at least for longer than ten minutes, someone had
to stay with me. Grandma Ryan missed a few of
the viewings at her Grandson Bobby's wake – her
own grandson – because she stayed with me. She
was our unofficial Grandma, one we never really
experienced because ours' passed away before we
had a chance to get to know them, at least for Deb
and myself. Dad's Mom went to the Maker when
I was three – meaning Deb never ever met her.
Grandma Baumbach was the only blood
Grandparent I knew. Grandma Ryan was
awesome in filling that empty void for all of us.

As we stood in front of the Burke home, we talked
about memories of this family that were so

intertwined with ours for so many decades. I recalled one summer day we all came home from our last day of school and for some reason every neighborhood kid seemed to have gathered on the Burke's front stoop. Bobby led us in singing 'No more teachers, no more books, no more teachers' dirty looks.' For some odd reason, that moment in time, never escaped me year after year when every one of my school years ended, and I would then relive it for my own children, who never knew why it meant so much to me. They probably long forgot this song, I didn't.

Strangely, as strong as the relationship was between Bobby and Dick, it wasn't the same for the rest of our brood. Jerry and I, while we played with Paul and Dennis, never had as close a relationship with them and we gradually lost touch over the years, only seeing them at their parents' funerals.

We talked about Paul, who ran track with the best of them. Tall and lanky, he was a sprinter. He would also read comic books – quite often. Sitting on their front stoop, Paul would read his comics and then laugh out loud at the humor they contained. He would have such a great time. He loudly cracked up laughing and it made me laugh as well whenever I would see or hear this. It was contagious! My favorite comics were Superman and Archie. Archie's crowd of the hot Veronica, the sweet Betty, tough guy Reggie, big Moose, and the always funny Jughead were the best!

Paul went onto be a teacher and raised two sons. And what did he name these children? - Why Bobby and Paul of course!

Dennis was also a runner. While he was closer in age to me, my vivid memory of him was his being really good at playing hide and seek. Or maybe he just didn't want me to find him. He also became a teacher.

We all lost touch.

The Burkes also had a weekend visitor who would come around about once a month. He was Mr. Burke's rotund brother Jeffrey. Jeffrey was a special kind of guy. Heavy set, he was probably one of the roundest people we ever met! He was such a sweet soul. He would tell us jokes and do tricks. One of these was catching the invisible ball in a brown paper bag; I used this one for years on my own kids and now grandkids. Thanks Jeffrey! You were a cool guy.

Our conversations rambled. We recalled the times when we would be sick, not feeling well at all. We would ask Mom to call the doctor, not any doctor, but our own neighborhood expert – Mrs. Burke. She knew more stuff about more things than anyone else we knew. Our own block's Hazel. She was strong, tough but very loving. And while no one asked where her training came from, no one ever had reason to question her knowledge.

We remembered the many holidays that we would share with the Burkes. Every Christmas Mrs. Burke would have her brothers and their families come visit for Christmas dinner, and we would then be invited in for dessert. We knew their families really well and we became friends with their kids. Dick and Jerry hung out with Jimmy who was Jack and Iris's son. He reminded us all of Ricky Nelson. I befriended Keith, Jim and Marie's son, and Deb became real close with Lisa, also from Jim and Marie. There was also an older sister of Jimmy's as well; whom I am sure was eyed by Dick!

Benny and Annette never had children. Benny was a Vice President at Emery Air Freight in Connecticut – years later the company was purchased by UPS. In his day, Benny was in charge of the purchasing of airline space for their large global business. This was a pretty impressive and tasking job.

Back in the summer of 1969, when I was in need of a summer job, Benny made a few calls and he single handedly launched my career in the logistics industry at Emery. Now, more than forty years later, I am still in it!

Benny passed away while at work in the company cafeteria, a legendary career well remembered. Years later, as I would venture to the corporate office, I would hear so many complementary tales about him. He paved the way for me. Thanks Benny! You made it so much easier.

Jim sadly lost his wife Marie early on, remarried and moved from Queens to be closer to his sister, Mary, on Long Island.

Jack was a Navy Vet. They lived in Connecticut. Jack and Iris had a certain class about them, not overstated, not boastful, but true real class. They had what John F. Kennedy had – charisma. Over time, Jack grew ill and ended up spending time in a hospital closer to his sister on LI.

For years, Dad often talked about moving to a new retirement center being built out in Eastern Long Island – called Leisure Village. It was really a solitary dream that was not shared by Mom who wanted to stay closer to her Williston Park 'roots.' Mom won.

The Burkes however, suddenly made a true life changing decision as they ventured into their elder years. They sold their Memory Lane home in the early '70's and moved to Leisure Village. This was one of the first true retirement communities catering to young seniors and it was quite the shock when they told us. Mom thought that perhaps they never got over the death of Bobby and needed a life change.

It also became another place for us to visit, but it wasn't the same. You cannot replace nearness with phone calls. They simply weren't next door anymore and Mom greatly missed her nightly chats, quick side door visits and more importantly, her 'sister.'

Both Mr. & Mrs. Burke passed away a number of years later. Mom made it to both of their services, Dad, stricken with Alzheimer's, could not.

However, in one of the rare times when Dad would 'reconnect' with us, during his long living wake, he would speak of the Burkes, citing things that surprised us all. We never knew how Dad would know of the things that would mysteriously come from his mouth. I recalled one quiet Saturday, about a year after Mr. Burke passed away, when Chris and I were 'watching' Dad, in order to give Mom a well deserved break; when he suddenly talked about how "sad Mary must be now that her husband Bob was gone."

The three of us had a short loving conversation, and Chris and I were astonished that Dad was speaking! For the first time we knew of in years, he was talking about a somewhat current event. I said, 'Dad, this is great, you're back!' Then as fast as he started talking he stopped. No more words.

That was the last I ever recall having had a true conversation with my father. For us it was obvious, the Burkes truly made a loving, living connection to our family.

Funny, for all the years of living next to the Burkes, Mr. Burke had something in common with Ozzie Nelson, of The Ozzie and Harriet TV Show. I never knew what he did for a living! I thought he had some role for Con Ed. I couldn't see him working on the street on a truck; rather I pictured him working in an office managing people. He was a brilliant, learned man, who would always get me going about how bad my Mets were and how they always lost. We had some invigorating conversations.

THE MCNEILS

We spoke about 'life after the Burkes,' their home and the family that moved in. Fittingly, next door also became another place for us to visit, but it wasn't really the same. The new people were very nice and eventually became extremely good friends with Mom and Dad. They helped tremendously during Dad's early stages of Alzheimer's, but it was indeed different. It was very different.

Bob and Jean McNeil moved in. A couple in their 40's–50's without children. What a rare thing for our block! The times they were a changing! They started making changes to the backyard. The Burke's backyard! It seemed real strange. Dad would initially look out our kitchen window and gaze sadly at what was going on. Seeing hedges replaced, seeing trees removed, seeing different cars in their driveway, seeing different people entering the house, Dad would question us about this. Perhaps this was the very start of his Alzheimer's taking hold.

Somehow, someway a new bond started to grow and the four of them became very good friends.

I told our gathering flock of family, which now numbered about fifteen, about the huge roll of white labels that Bob gave Chris and me back in 1975. It was a HUGE roll of labels....about the size of a round wash basket. We never knew why Bob gave it to us, but over the years Chris and I would use them to label our children's school books and many, many other things. Now, some 35 years later, we still have many labels left on the roll! This thing was like a tub of cheese from Holland!

They both last for years and improve with age!

Jean stayed close with Mom, and eventually she too moved, to Westchester County. We thought she moved to be nearer to her sister. As she went about clearing her home, she came across a lovely coffee table with a slate insert that she could not move with her. She wanted to sell it and knew Chris and I always liked it. Jean gave us an offer we couldn't refuse and it still serves prominently in our living room years later.

Jean had a very hearty laugh and was really good for Mom and Dad, especially for Mom as Dad grew deeper and deeper into the throes of Alzheimer's.

Mom stayed in touched with Jean over the years and her's was one of the phone calls that we sadly had to make upon Mom's passing. Oddly, we never asked what had happened to Bob. But we still have a lot of those labels.

The Burkes taught me Family Values. The McNeils taught me Kindness. We then went walked a few feet next door to ....our home.

The Bridge to our Home via Mom and Dad's First Home

Perhaps some background music please – how about George M Cohan's:

"Over There".

It was 1941 and our country was at war, the one called The Big One. Mom and Dad met in 1939, courted, married, moved from each others' homes. Dad was from Corona, in the area near the World's Fair of 1939 and 1964/5, and close to what would become Shea Stadium / Citi Field, the home of the Mets. Mom was from the Bronx.

Dad was third from the bottom of a family of 11 children, including a brother Charlie, who passed away on Christmas Eve at the age of five from 'The Fever.' Mom was also in the middle of a family of five, including a brother named Bernard, who passed away at the age of five from 'The

Fever.' It was a sad but prevalent ailment among youngsters early in the 20th Century. I believe they both passed in 1910. It was an oddity that both Mom and Dad shared. I never actually knew what that fever really was all about but there was one thing that I did know, I didn't want to catch it!

The young couple found an apartment for the new life they were building together. It would be in Queens. In a hamlet called Elmhurst. Dad brought his belongings, probably a baseball mitt, some underwear, some corny jokes and a fedora or two. (I've been told he looked dashing in his fedora)! Mom didn't have much to bring with her except for a few treasured items, such as her Mom's glass Irish lamp which has become a family heirloom, maintained by Deb to this day and a few other very personal attachments. Two of whom were her younger brother and sister: James and Estelle.

Elmhurst

Tragically, the day Mom and Dad's Wedding Announcements were mailed out by Mom's Mom, Grandmother Sarah Smith, Grandma had an embolism and died instantly, never to see her daughter get married. In an era before cell phones and beepers, Mom went to work that day, May 10, 1941, only to return in the evening to a house full of people scurrying around in true anguish and found her Mom dead.

She never again saw her Mom alive after their morning kiss goodbye.

Mom's Dad had passed away years earlier, while she was in her teens. Her eldest brother John married a girl from the Gamble family, of the Proctor and Gamble Company. They had two sons, born on the exact same day a few years apart. John launched a successful career with a National Newspaper Chain, Scripps Howard, in Cincinnati, Ohio.

James and Estelle, both single, lived at home with Mom and their Mom. Once their Mom died, they had no place to go. In the apartment house that the family called home, Grandma was the employed superintendent. She was responsible for insuring the tenants' apartments were in working order. For that, she received her apartment and a small stipend. When she passed on, their home went away. The three of them, collectively would have to start paying the rent together but Mom was about to get married. So it was that Dad took them in along with his bride to their new apartment, a tiny one bedroom unit in Elmhurst. It was small, very small. Along with his brother in law, our Uncle John Brutschy, Dad divided the three small rooms as best they could so that the four of them could get some sense of privacy. While they didn't have a TV set, they listened to their RCA Victrola Radio and certainly played lots of Dad's favorite card game: pinochle!

Ironically, Uncle John later worked on developing a patent with the US Government, while working for a major defense contractor, and legend has it, his patent was related to portable expanded room construction. He had experience!

Mom and Dad's Wedding Day, June 1, 1941
Estelle, Mom, Dad and Uncle Johnny
Mom never got to wear her gown

Our Uncle Jim

James stayed with the newlyweds and Estelle until the time when Dick was born and they had the obvious need for more space. He moved to Kentucky, took a job selling Norcross Greeting Cards and sadly, suddenly passed away due to asphyxiation in 1951.

We never learned too much about what happened, but we knew it was tragic. Mom and Dad went by train to Louisville, Kentucky, met up with Uncle John, and they brought his body back home to be buried 'near' his home in New York's St John's Cemetery.

Dick would have the greatest memories of Uncle Jim. He bought 'his boys' our famous airplane tricycle. It was passed down from Dick to Jerry to me, however somehow I must have had a crash landing while flying it since it never made it to Deb! Too bad, I remember feeling so cool flying (driving) this plane all over our block as a kid. No one else had one! We felt very special having this airplane!

My memories, if one can call them that, of Uncle Jim were threefold (hey, remember I was only two when he left us).

1. The Airplane Tricycle – though I do not actually recall Uncle Jim

2. Whenever the Movie "Yankee Doodle Dandy" was on television, (usually on July 4th), Mom would say that Jimmy Cagney looked just like her younger brother Jim. In fact any time any Jimmy Cagney movie was on Mom would say that!

3. $500. The story went that Uncle Jim really took a liking to Dick and took very good care of him while he was alive. Hey, he bought him that great airplane! By the time Jerry and I arrived, we lived far away from him. To make up for this, he put some money into an account for each of us. For some reason, I always remember it being $500. It probably started out as $100 back in 1950. But Mom and Dad would have to go every year or so to some courthouse in Queens, NY to fill out papers for this money, which we would receive when we turned 21. I remembered one particular time, Jerry and I discussed these court visits in our basement. It went something like this:

The Following is a Life Recreation:

Jerry: "Why do you think Mom and Dad have to go to court all the time and it's only about us, and Not about Dick?"

Me: "Geesh, I don't know, what do you think?"

Jerry: "Well, courts are serious business, they have to talk to a judge and all that stuff."

Me: "Geesh ,Wow!"

Jerry; "I wonder if we were adopted and Dick wasn't!"

Me: "Geesh, you think so?"

Jerry: "Well, you are blonde, I am brown haired and Dick has dark hair – what do you think?"

Me: "Geesh, I don't know, I didn't know we were adopted!"

Both of us: "MOM!"

Dick: "It's my Airplane!"

Mom: "Ron you have my eyes, Jerry you have your fathers!"

Me: "Huh? Geesh!"

Our Beloved Estelle
ONE OF A KIND, AN INCREDIBLY SPECIAL AUNT AND AN EVEN BETTER PERSON

While Jerry was born in the mid '40's and I came along a few years later, Estelle stayed with our growing family as we all moved from Elmhurst to Williston Park in 1952. We bought our own house! Estelle lived with us until the mid '50's when Deb was born. I always said, I threw Uncle Jim out and Deb threw Estelle out!

In essence, Estelle was the aunt who was so many things to us. An incredibly supportive and loving 'Big Sister'; a 'young and vibrant Grandmother like personality,' a loving relative who treated 'her kids' always special, we were always right, she hugged us, kissed us, bought us gifts, took us on trips. She was 'Our Best Friend' and an Amazing Confidante to us all. Quite simply, she was our Estelle. We never ever called her Aunt Estelle, but our Estelle.

The beauty of life consists of the people who enter it and the ones who make a difference in others lives. The sadness is when these people leave, especially when it is far too early. Life can be fair, unfair, just, or unjust.

We were all blessed with Estelle. In fact, it is my firm belief, that everyone needs an Estelle in their life. While she has never left our loving emotional world, which is so full of so many incredible memories, she sadly left our earthly world in 1979 victimized by cancer, a disease she valiantly fought for years. Estelle's last year was a long arduous period, one which my loving wife Chris endured throughout her nine month pregnancy, because I would often leave our home to run to the hospital or to Mom and Dad's to see Estelle, each time thinking it was for the last time.

Upon Estelle's passing, Mom took exception to the formality and description on her death certificate, which similar to Dad's simply listed: Cause of Death: Heart Failure. How crazy, sure her heart may have given out due to exhaustion but her death was from cancer, plain and simple, as Dad's was from Alzheimer's.

The beauty of Estelle was her being Estelle. She would go out of her way to make time for us. She would plan her schedule around ours. She would take us on annual Christmas shopping trips to New York City – and the majority of the money we spent as we bought 'our' gifts to give other members of our family was hers.

Deb once had a class project in which the students were requested to draw a picture of their family. Having known our family, the teacher questioned Deb's drawing, since it showed seven people, as opposed to our six.

'Who is this tall woman?' asked the teacher of Deb. 'Oh,' Deb said, 'that's Estelle, she's my big sister!'

Estelle taught all of us how to maneuver the New York City subway system and when I got older, I was allowed to travel it alone to meet her. We all went to a number of places in the city, such as Radio City, museums, playgrounds and the movies. My favorite two dates with Estelle were "Lady and the Tramp" and "Breakfast at Tiffany's."

I was excited when my wife Chris and I returned the favor to Estelle on one of her birthdays, when we took her to see Yul Brenner in "The King and I" followed by dinner. The tables turned and I was so glad we did this....for she was failing and fading fast.

As we got older, Estelle would have us bring our dates to her apartment for a romantic dinner. Sounds odd, right, taking a date to your aunt's for a romantic dinner! But Estelle would do it up right and have us look so special in front of the girls we would bring to her home.

She would lend (give) us money; she would help us financially when we would buy our first car; she was there when we got in trouble and not tell Mom or Dad; she was cool and would give us unconditional advice when we needed someone to simply listen. Bottom line, her love for us was never ending as she was always, always there for us. Simply said, she was our Estelle.

Mom and her baby sister Estelle on a horse e 1922

I remembered Estelle taking me and our cousin Mike, who is our Uncle John's son, to New York City for a show and dinner. I recalled being really full from dinner, but I so wanted this incredibly huge dessert. I can still recall Estelle ordering it for me. When it came, I simply could not eat it. Rather than say, 'you should have known better and not have ordered it,' Estelle simply said, 'that's not a problem, your eyes were bigger than your stomach! I bet you'll save room and eat it the next time.' Her nephews and niece could not rock her!

My handwriting was never good. It was surely the one subject I continually had problems with in grade school, my lowest grades by far. Estelle's was not too good either. When I would complain about this she would turn to me and simply say, 'what are you worried about, bad penmanship is a true sign of intelligence!'

When she moved away, she knew she would need to drive so she went for a driver's license, passed the test and bought a car, a small green one. However, she always had an odd fear of making left turns. She would drive from Queens to our house and complained about how long the trip would take because she could only make right turns! Realizing this wouldn't work, she eventually sold the car; commuting by bus and train to our house. As she got older and ill, we would drive her to and from our home.

Estelle never married, but she got close twice. She was engaged years before we were born, but she said as they got nearer to the 'Day' she felt it wouldn't work out and broke off the engagement. It was an area that was never really a topic of conversation. So we didn't pursue it.

Romance came again to Estelle years later when Mom and Dad decided to have their kitchen remodeled. A local shop owner and widower named Mr. Johnson would come to our home for measurements, etc. He came quite often and it would normally be when Estelle was visiting for the weekend. Estelle's visits were usually every other weekend at that time. The kitchen measurements would always encounter a running delay and need to be rescheduled – for two weeks later, on a weekend when Estelle was visiting. Mr. Johnson was a cool shrewd dude!

Eventually they dated, and the couple appeared to be serious. We were all rooting for it; because they appeared so great together. Estelle, the beautiful red head who looked a lot like Lucille Ball, and Mr. Johnson, the dashing entrepreneur who looked like Clark Gable. Something happened however, and they suddenly broke up, and this too was never discussed. Oddly, she was there for us, but, looking back, it appears that we, the kids, were not there for her! Mom and Estelle had countless phone calls, not that we knew what they were about.

When Deb was born, Estelle moved out of the

small corner bedroom in the front of our house back to Queens.   She returned to the Elmhurst area, very close to the apartment she had once shared with Mom and Dad.   Her old room was then taken over by Dick, which caused a whole welcome ripple effect of sudden childhood maturity, with me actually getting out of Mom and Dad's room and into a kid's bedroom to share with Jerry.   Poor Jerry never knew what hit him! But at six, I was due for a move!

Estelle's first apartment was a very small studio, with a Murphy bed – a bed that was hidden in the wall which she would magically bring down when she wanted to go to sleep. We thought it was so cool.   We never realized it also meant her living space was therefore very limited. Her kitchen was like a small closet, but it became an anchor of Estelle's home and we would long for our visits to her, which were often.

We would be thrilled to ride in her elevator, watching the metal scissor like bars come apart from the wall when you opened the elevator door. But it was more exciting to be the one selected to put her garbage in the special hallway chute that gave it a ride down the five flights to an incinerator somewhere below!

Over the course of time, Estelle would move up, not to the East Side, but to larger and larger apartments in Queens.   Her financial situation must have moved up as well, since she would decorate with custom made furniture. She had fancy detailed painted murals of San Francisco Bay on her bar wall which lit up at night with an expensive blue light that was hidden in the ceiling. When lit, you felt like you were actually overlooking the Golden Gate Bridge!

Her bar and benches were made by a local master carpenter. The handiwork was most creative and tasteful, a Spanish motif, pieces of which still remain in our immediate and extended families today. One Christmas, when I was about 18, I gave Estelle a rather large statue of Don Quixote, to complement the look. I always loved The Impossible Dream and knew he would fit right in, to both Estelle's ambience and her personal view of life. While 'Don' still looks for a new home, I store him and all of his remaining dreams in my garage!

Estelle would expand her surroundings and find many wonderful friends in her new neighborhoods. Single and widowed women became her treasured gal pals. There were a lot of them and our family would become best friends with these lovely ladies and their families as well. People such as Kay, Lucille, and Millie and near the end of her life, Dad's brother Eddie's widow, Aunt Marie, who lived a few homes away from Estelle, joined her circle of life. Before the "Mary Tyler Moore Show", Estelle was our own Mary.

Estelle loved to travel and with her friend Helen, they would tour the American landscape with trips to places such as Las Vegas, Orlando, (before there was a Disney World), New York City, staying at the Americana Hotel, and also cruised on her favorite ship - The Cruise to Nowhere!

We would celebrate Estelle, obviously along with Mom on Mother's Day. But while she too would receive a corsage and a gift, she really deserved her own day. She deserved an Estelle Day!

When I was admitted to the hospital due to my scoliosis, she knew it would be for months before I would come home. I knew every Sunday there would be at least two visitors at my bedside, Mom and Estelle. On the six Sunday's that Dad would work out of seven, Estelle and Mom would take the train. The 140 mile roundtrip train ride, which was combined with a taxi was taken by Estelle week after week. Somehow, she would meet Mom along the route and they would ride together from Mineola and then walk or cab it through the hills of Port Jefferson to my hospital.

The first Sunday she visited, she wanted me to have my own TV in my room, so she bought me a small set to bring to my hospital room. As she brought it in, security made her take it out. For whatever reason back then it wasn't allowed, and TV wasn't available either. She was ticked!

When I was finally released, Estelle would take me to see my love - Met games at Shea Stadium! We always had great seats. She would talk to her bosses who owned a fashion house in the garment area, called Schwatt Brothers. The brothers admired and appreciated their bookkeeper, Estelle. Their bookkeeper loved her job. Quite often they would spring for box seat tickets for both of us to go to games. I was thrilled to be able to be up front and personal and see games from a view I never imagined existed!

I remembered one particular player event, Family Day, I had to pee so I went to the Shea Stadium First Level bathroom and was actually on the same line as the players' sons, all wearing their dad's uniforms. I could tell because no one wore 'team jerseys' back then, it wasn't the marketing bonanza it is now. It may seem odd, it may seem strange, but to me, this was surreal. I was standing in the stall next to Met pitching great Al Jackson's son! Amazing, Amazing! Amazing! Can life get better! I was taking a leak next to a Mets player's kid!

Estelle had told her bosses how I had to lie down on my back, both in the hospital and while at home for months on end. The Schwatt's figured it would be rough and tough for the back of my head. They took a huge piece of natural lambskin, measured about four feet square and gave it to Estelle for me to lie my head on. It still sits on the chair in my home office, and is still soft, so many years later!

On Saturday evenings, when we were kids, we would gather around our dining room table with Estelle and play either board games or cards, such as Canasta, Hearts, or whatever new game she learned from one of her many trips. If Dad joined in, the game turned to Pinochle.

We would have our soda and she would have her glass of beer. After work, Estelle would enjoy her favorite drink, a Manhattan. While she would enjoy the adult beverage, none of us ever saw or heard of her ever abusing it. It wasn't the same for cigarettes however.

In the mid seventies, Estelle found a lump on her breast and she chose to ignore it. She finally told Mom and they would discuss this at length. After Mom's persuading, she finally decided to go to a doctor to check it out. The doctor wanted Estelle to have it removed at Sloan Kettering Hospital in Manhattan. It was the premier hospital for cancer at the time. Mom, Dad and I went with Estelle to have her admitted. It was a cool clear Sunday in the fall. Suddenly, as we were walking in, Estelle decided to walk out.

She wanted to go home and no matter how hard and long we tried to convince her otherwise, we had to take her home.

This was a tough time for Mom, who wanted so much to have Estelle take care of herself. A few months went by and finally Estelle agreed to take care of the matter and return to the hospital. I remembered waiting to see a reenactment of Estelle's leaving, but it didn't happen. Fortunately, she had the surgery. Unfortunately the news was not good.

Estelle's doctor was the number one rated breast surgeon in NY at that time. He was on the news quite a lot, as breast cancer was fast becoming a major topic. It got a tremendous push in the public eye when in 1974, President Gerald Ford's wife, Betty, announced that she had breast cancer. Estelle's surgery was quick, but when the doctor called us in to talk to us he said he had to perform a double mastectomy because it was cancer.

We all went in to see her quite often. For me, it was somewhat easy, as I worked in the city, and would see her at lunch or after work. For Mom and Dad it was much more of a trek, but they did it religiously.

Estelle fought the disease, worked on her exercises, especially the little pink ball she had to squeeze in her hand countless times every day to regain muscle strength. Once home in her apartment, she had to go back and forth to the hospital for treatment. She would take cabs, Lindy's car service, or we would drive her. Her expenses were high.

It was shortly after that, for whatever reason, Estelle decided to change jobs and went to work for a new garment house. It didn't make sense to us, but obviously it did to Estelle and she didn't really share the details with the kids, hopefully she did with Mom. But after missing so much work, her new employer laid her off. Business can be so cruel. But at the end of the day, these people didn't really know Estelle and they were a small company who could not afford her many absences, that's at least what she told us. She then proceeded to work many odd office jobs wherever she could find work, in between her many hospital visits.

Estelle seemed like she was beating the cancer. I remembered Mom having a large family dinner the night of Estelle's five year cancer free anniversary, which was a big thing back then. Making it to five years without the disease was something to celebrate. So we had a toast to her health.

Unfortunately, the celebration did not last long after that as her cancer started coming out of remission and took aim at Estelle's body. It was not a happy time. But we all had hope, we always had hope and many prayers.

Finally the day came when we had to move Estelle

out of her last apartment. It was tough. Deb was away in school, so Chris, Mom, Dad, and I went for the final move to bring Estelle back to Mom and Dad's home. Basically, while no one ever said it, it was to come home for her final ride. The best part of that day was the joy surrounding Chris' pregnancy with our son Jim. Estelle talked and talked about the pregnancy and about the newly elected Pope, a Polish Cardinal who broke a long run of Italian Pontiffs. Estelle was so proud for Chris and her family who are Polish.

Estelle came home to a bedroom set up in Mom and Dad's dining room. She was frail. She was losing weight and her stability, but not her mind or her spirit. It was during that period when Deb needed a car. Estelle looked for money to help her buy it. Somehow she found it. She never stopped giving.

Estelle waited anxiously for Jerry to move into his new house with Elaine and their three boys. She promised them that she would visit. She did.

Estelle wanted so much to see our baby born. Upon his birth, he had some serious medical issues, since Estelle was bedridden at home she surely could not visit, but she could pray, which she did. As Chris was still in her room in maternity at one hospital and our newborn son was in another hospital, I spent the night before his surgery in Mom and Dad's home as it was nearer to his location. Estelle was also there and she gave me loving words of encouragement. It worked and our baby's surgery was successful.

Unexpectedly, I took both Chris and our newborn baby home early on Saturday, the 24th of December. As we drove away from the hospital, we looked at each other with a similar thought. You know how married couples can think the same thing without talking? We both knew we had to stop at Mom and Dad's so Estelle could see her newest grand nephew. She had waited anxiously for this moment and we both wanted to fulfill this wish.

When we entered the house, she was thrilled. We were nervous but delighted, as Estelle so much wanted to hold him. We propped her up in her bed and laid Jim in her arms. She gingerly and lovingly held our baby James. Estelle had promised she would wait for our Jim to be born and she wanted so much to see him, touch him, and hold him. She kept her promise.

Estelle's body was very brittle. A few days after meeting Jim, just before New Year's Eve, while simply moving in bed, she somehow broke a leg. She had to be taken to the hospital. She never came home, passing away a short time later.

This period was tough on all the members of our family, especially to my wife, who just days earlier, gave birth to our baby who two days later had to be taken away from her and be driven in an ambulance for neuro-surgery. She was also recovering from her own emergency C section and living with a husband who was running back and forth to visit his Aunt who was dying. I am forever grateful for the compassion and love Chris gave me as I met my family at the hospital countless times to see Estelle. Ironically, on the one day I didn't visit, for whatever reason, that was the day Estelle passed.

Estelle knew she had to leave us. Her job was done. At her wake and funeral, it was a cause for celebration, of both Estelle's life and our baby. Newborns can do that. So in essence, the joy of our infant son's birth helped somewhat to ease the pain of Estelle's death.

She was and is truly, one of the most beloved and very special people in my life.

A few months before Estelle passed away, I was a pall bearer at my friend Fred's father's funeral. I had never been to a grave side burial service before and attended this with their family members and close friends. The emotions of the moment got to me and I broke down in tears. I was the one who had to be consoled. A short time later, composed, I drove away, alone. But for obvious reasons, I could not stop thinking of Estelle, who was still alive but surely not doing well. So I drove directly to visit her. Something told me that I needed to spend time with her that day. As I approached her, I thought I would not tell her what just occurred, but when we met, she knew something was wrong and we discussed it. She was once again ever so kind to me.

I remembered telling Estelle that someday I wanted to write a book about her life, her many successes, her challenges and her battle with cancer. I shared the hopeful title with her: One Valiant Life. Though I don't know if the book will ever be put to paper, I know one thing for certain, that for the four of us, who grew up having the wonderment of Estelle being such a loving, instrumental and indelible part of our lives, her memory is one that we forever cherish and are most thankful that we were all given the most loving gift of Estelle.

Estelle taught me so many values by her words and actions; one that has stood out is Positive Reinforcement.

Estelle watching us play in the park ⓔ *1958*

THE GATES

Our home was between the Burkes and the Gates. At the time of our journey, Mrs. Gates, Flora, still lived at home, along with her youngest son Chad.

Their children: Kyle, Scott and Adam had all moved on. Mr. Gates, Ben, sadly passed away of a heart attack a few years back, I believe on the evening of one of our many block parties.

Our Search for a New Home

It was the summer of '52, Frank and Loretta decided to leave their small apartment and make the move that many others had done before them – to what was the fastest growing county in America – Nassau County. They had real estate people do their homework for them and searched for our new home. Years later, it became a routine family pastime for Dad to show us the homes they didn't choose. I recalled two that were in this group, one on Horton Highway; truly not a highway by any means except for its name and another in a far away section of Mineola, real near the E.J. Korvette's store about three miles away.

I used to wonder what life would have been like if we would have moved there instead. That was me, I would think of those types of things! Some pondered, I wondered.

Besides using real estate professionals, Mom and Dad also did their new home research by checking with their inner circle, which as you have seen, was the Burkes and the Murrays, who led them to look at the available house on Memory Lane.

What happened when they first arrived truly became one of our life's quinkydinks! As Mom and Dad were walking in the backyard, checking out the garage and the 'spacious' but limited grounds, next door they saw a red haired lady. Mom and Flora Gates eyes met, could it be, amazing, yes! Two cousins reunited!

Yes we were related to the Gates. Mom's Mom was Sarah Brady. Flora Gates father was also a Brady. To make a long lineage short, they had the same great-grandparents. In the long path of ancestry and however the world of cousins 'once removed' works, the woman next door was indeed Mom's cousin!

Mrs. Gates would tell me years later, how she was

tasked with watching me and more importantly hold me as my two year old personality was prone to misbehave. This helped Mom and Dad peacefully inspect the house while they were negotiating the deal. Hey, give me a break, I was not yet three!

While the Gates were related to us, and Mom's immediate and extended family was indeed small, compared to Dad's (he was one of eleven), our family ties didn't really come together until years later when our true family bonds took place. Family links can be somewhat stronger than neighborly ones. One thought that I recalled was that her son Scott always felt we should have addressed our parents as Aunt and Uncle. For whatever reason, it never happened. Perhaps it just didn't seem right at the time. Sorry Scott! Looking back, perhaps we should have taken your advice.

The Gates had a most characteristic archway which led to their side door. It was made of white brick which was attached to the house. During the summer, it would be covered with beautiful red roses. Their house was painted green with white trim. They, like us and all the others on Memory Lane, had a long one car pebbled driveway.

For the most part, all of the kids on the block were Catholic and most of us went to our local Catholic School, St. Aidan's, which was 9/10th of a mile away from our home. That tenth of a mile was a very important factor since one had to be a minimum of one mile away to get a school bus for grades three and up. So it meant we had to walk, ride a bike, or if was a rainy day and we were lucky, we would all cram inside the Gates' car.

I recalled one of their first cars was a very large green machine. It was truly heavy metal before Heavy Metal became what it is today! In addition, Mrs. Gates was somewhat unique in that she actually had a driver's license and drove a car which was an awesome thing back then. I believe she was one of the first Moms to drive in our neighborhood. On those rainy days, she would pack us all in the car and drive us to school. Seat belts? Car Seats? Hmmm, not back then! Somehow, someway, we made sure we all fit in her car!

School Days

It felt like 85% of the kids on our block went to St. Aidan's; the rest went to Cross Street, the public school for grades one to five. The Catholic school boys wore brown pants, a tan shirt and a brown tie with the famous SAS embroidered on it. Girls, besides wearing the compulsory monthly colored bow on their hair, wore a plaid green skirt with a white blouse.

We had nuns teach us, lots of them, all dressed in their black habit with their tall white and black pointed hat. We often wondered if they had hair under there or if they had to take the vow of baldness when they became a nun. They were members of the Sisters of Charity order and we prayed daily for the beatification of their founder, now St. Elizabeth Ann Seton. We believed we had a lot to do with the Pope making his positive final decision.

The nuns were tough but they had to be. They had a lot of kids in the school! The Catholics seemed to dominate Williston Park and everyone had a bunch of tykes! Sex education was not part of the curriculum. We thought if a Dad so much as winked at a Mom, she would get pregnant. There must have been a lot of winking! One of the first grade classrooms was managed by dear Sister Leone, who looked like she was about 110 years old. Scary thing was stories were told of her being really old years before we got there, and years later, she would still be teaching, still looking the same...110 years old. She was singlehandedly the very best at teaching us how to read. Masterful. But you better not erase too hard or it would cost you a nickel if you rubbed a hole in the paper. I guess paper was hard to come by back then or eraser heads. While she was a great teacher, she also frightened me a little bit and I would have personal emergency 'accidents,' if you know what I mean. Frustrated she would call my oldest brother, Dick, down from eighth grade to talk to me about bladder control! She would confuse my often raised hand, thinking I knew the answer to her questions with my incessant requests to be excused. Finally, she gave me a special rule, whenever I had to go, I could just get up and leave, no questions asked. We became friends after that and years later when I met her again at an alumni affair, (I was then a young adult, she was retired but she still looked like she was 110), we shared a few good laughs.

Second grade was a blast, one of my friends, Richie Ziske's mom was my teacher and she was the most blessed teacher a child could ever ask for. I don't recall having had many bladder issues in this grade, but my special rule still existed so perhaps that took care of the problem. I enjoyed this grade a lot and it grew more special because of all of our training for our First Confession and First Communion. Both went very well for me. However prior to both, stories would abound about possible issues with what the priest would say in their special chamber; what sins we needed to confess; what was a mortal sin vs. what was a venial sin; about receiving the Host; concerns about throwing up; choking; etc. Quite a lot for a seven year old's bladder to handle you might say. But I survived and did quite well. We all were verbally tested by our pastor, Father Lowe, who was most kind, had our First Confession, mine was with Father Kirwin and as for the receiving the Host, I did it ever so well! Thanks Mrs. Ziske!

My third grade class had a lot of kids in it. I think it was 83 students, that's right, 83! And it was one nun, no aide! Sister Virginia Mary should have been canonized for what she did. That was the first place where I ever saw index cards. She would have all of our names on these lined pieces of hard paper, and then meticulously had them set up in a file box on her big desk, which sat boldly in front of the room. She would use them to get to know us. It worked!

On the very last day of class, when you received your final report card, you would also find out what classroom / teacher you would have the following year. Kids would gather together as best we could as we filed out of school for the summer comparing notes. Were we with our friends, or did they break us all up? Moms would buzz the phone party lines checking out to see if their friends would also be together.

Fourth grade for me meant I would have a lay teacher, Mrs. Minute, whom I believed got sick midway during the year. I appeared to be quite fortunate having had her because I missed not having the nun who had the reputation of being the toughest teacher in the school, Sister Catherine William. Stories were told of her being extremely stern. Supposedly her right index finger could poke a hole right through your chest! In her defense however, my friends who got her, never talked about her in a negative way, in fact, they all loved her. Guess all she needed was a good PR Agent!

My memories of fifth grade, that I cared to share and that still linger, were threefold.

One day, early in the school year, I was selected to be part of the group that got to go to the auditorium and bring the milk to our classroom. It came in those tiny little containers that you had to carefully pry open at the top seams so they wouldn't leak. It took about 15 minutes to get those darned things opened and I always seemed to open the wrong end. Well this particular day, off I went with three other kids to get the day's supply of milk for our class. When I returned the empty cases with the other kids, I met a friend from the other fifth grade class and we started talking. It caused me to be late. I knew we had a major test that we had to take, so I rushed back, alone. Not seeing the three other kids, whom I assumed ran ahead of me; I ran up the stairs to my classroom, opened the door, ran down the aisle to my seat and what did I see, but some other kid sitting in my desk! I was ticked. Why are you sitting in my seat I asked! Then I noticed, this kid wasn't even in my class. He even seemed smaller than my fellow classmates! What was going on? Then I suddenly realized. I only went up one flight of stairs, meaning I was one floor below my classroom. Mine was on the second floor and here I was on the first! Feeling like a complete fool, I said nothing, their teacher never saw me, or if she did, she said nothing, and I quickly ran out back up the stairs to my classroom...and silently sat in my desk for the test! No one said a word....and I breathed a sigh of silent relief!

I also never asked to do milk duty again.

A few weeks later, while still in fifth grade, for whatever reason the kid who sat behind me jokingly hit me on the head with a notebook when I got a question wrong. It was before lunchtime and I wasn't expecting it, nor was my hungry growling stomach. Suddenly and loudly I let out the loudest fart. If nothing else, it changed the attention from my wrong answer to a room full of laughter.

During the month of May of fifth Grade, I decided I would go to Mass every day and accomplished this by

Williston Park Public Library

riding my bicycle to church before school. At the end of May, being it was the month dedicated to Mary, Jesus' Mother, there would an annual crowning of the Blessed Virgin Mary across the street in the Boys' School yard. It was a really big deal. There would be a huge procession with the whole school marching across the street. All the priests and teachers were to be involved. One morning the PA came on in on classroom and our Principal started talking saying she would soon make a major announcement. Our class had been acting up and our teacher was getting frustrated and she said if we don't calm down we won't be allowed to attend the crowning.

Suddenly the Principal called my name over the loudspeaker and asked me to come to the office. I was thinking perhaps I was in trouble, maybe I was still getting caught up in the eraser issue of first grade, or they were going to rescind my right of going to the bathroom whenever I felt the need to. Sweating, I walked the hallway, with some girl chosen to accompany me. When we got there, the Principal and some parish priests greeted us and congratulated me saying that they put all of the names of the students who went to daily Mass into a bucket and I was selected to crown Mary! It was awesome! Excited we both went back to our classroom to make the news public to our teacher and fellow classmates. Sister Francis Damien was thrilled and said to the class that they lucked out because of me ….now they would definitely march in the procession!

Mom and Dad came to the crowning. Dad took off

Williston Park Public Library

from work and filmed it. It was perhaps my brightest shining moment in grammar school!

On Wednesday's we would happily get to leave school early because the public school kids would come to our school to use our classrooms for CCD, commonly called religious instructions. We loved this because it meant we always had one day in the middle of the week when we could get out early, go home and play. Certainly not all the parents enjoyed it as much as the kids did! Due to the heavy influx of the good nuns in our school, I assumed that our teachers became their teachers as well. We felt bad for the public school kids who were being schooled while we were set free!

In sixth grade, perhaps due to a rapid level of rising hormones, the boys left the girls and the nuns to move across the street to the 'Boys' School, taught by the Franciscan Brothers. They were a cool bunch of men who could relate to the guys. They were sports enthusiasts, musically inclined, high moral fiber and generally excellent teachers. They also taught us to grow up but I may have taken it a bit farther than what was intended. Two people I met that year have had a profound influence on my life. One was a most strict and demanding teacher, Brother Finian, who became an incredible supporter of mine throughout my spinal fusion journey. He visited me often, offered incredible words of wisdom and gave me a most beloved crucifix of Jesus which still hangs on my office wall. The other was one of my closest friends, Fred Emken, who transferred to St. Aidan's in the sixth grade. I shared vivid memories of the day Brother Finian had Fred

*stand in front of our class and introduced him to us all.
I thought about how difficult it must have been to be the
new kid when all the others have been together for some
six years. While we did not become strong friends until
years later, we have shared many memories of middle
school, high school and college which moved the
relationship from friendship into being treated like
members of each others' family.*

*Brother Jacques became one of our teachers in the
seventh grade. He was a highly educated, ever loving
and harmless man who had the sad distinction of
looking a little different than others. He had somewhat
drooping lips with sad eyes to go with them. This poor
man went through hell with our class. Ashamed to say,
but what seemed quite funny back then grew into
embarrassing behavior which I truly regretted as I grew
older. The Franciscans wore a heavy brown robe with a
white tassel and a large open hood as their daily garb.
Brother Jacques became the object of many a joke from
our class. Such as throwing spit balls into his hood
when his back was turned from us, or we would merge
desks together and lock him between two rows as he
walked through the classroom.   Perhaps the most
organized was our class bombs. Particularly during
seventh grade, our country was living through the Bay
of Pigs Invasion, the Cuban Missile Crisis and the ever
long never thawed Cold War. We were constantly
advised that we were on the brink of a major world war
and we all had to be ready for a possible attack. Homes
had bomb shelters stocked with canned foods and
supplies, ours was in our basement. Dad made sure of*

that. In school, we would have numerous surprise drills where we were told to put our heads on the desk, or even go below the desk as preparation for protection from the nuclear bombs that were said would come from above.

The boys in our class played off of that and somehow we could start our own chain of bomb scares by systematically dropping a large text book, milliseconds apart, so it would sound like multiple bombs were falling. Then we would all jump out of our desks and hide for cover underneath them. Rarely however, did Brother Jacques get upset. He had the patience of a saint.

I started the year joining in on the mischievous fun, and remembered during Lent tempting him with ice cream treats knowing he had to fast. Somehow, towards the end of that school year, it got to me, I felt bad and sorry for how we had treated him and I would go and talk to the good brother and actually got to know him quite well. He was a real pleasure, most learned and a very nice guy who liked sports, which was a joy we shared.

Oddly enough, in a most bizarre twist, our paths would cross twice more in life. During my courtship with my wife Chris, I learned that he was a cousin of one of her family's dearest friends. A few years later, it became even more bizarre. As Dad was in his nursing home, losing his long battle to Alzheimer's, Brother Jacques was a few doors down the hallway, fighting his own health issues. He and Dad passed away a few weeks apart. So sorry Brother Jacques!

Sixth grade was supposed to show a level of maturation. I had always had a temper which I pretty much kept under control. I was therefore pretty low key and never wanted to cause a scene, until I had an issue with a tough seventh grader who would always bug me in the playground. I never knew why, but he would make fun of me and harass me during lunch time. It really annoyed me. One of the teachers told me I needed to stand up to him and let him know I wouldn't take it. I took this to heart and the next day, when this Billy Bully came over to me to start his daily rant, I let him have it with a vocal display of displeasure about his attitude and how I wasn't going to take it anymore and if he kept it up, I would let him have it. (I never explained what 'it' was). He looked at me in silent awe and when I finished, he simply said, "Sorry Man, no offense intended." He never bothered me again. Ironically we then became friends. Weird!

That wasn't so true of my coming of age with a fellow classmate when we were in seventh grade together. He was one of the guys in our class who was the heart throb of the girls. He had the James Dean looks, was a top athlete in the class, one of the smartest kids and possessed a true gift of charisma. We were friends, but it was more like you would be thrilled to be in his inner circle. One particular lunch period, he started bragging, I always hated bragging, and he went on and on about something about him vs. me. Finally I had had enough and went over to him and told him to stop it. He didn't so I hit him. He went down and the other kids all looked on in wonder. As he got up, he said nothing, just walked away. No one ever reported me to the teachers. I always thought he was too embarrassed to publicize it and perhaps the other kids were in shock but glad that I did what I did. I think I hurt his pride more than his body.

Over the course of these three years, most of the guys liked our new school, though I recalled some would get in trouble with Brother Finian for still longing for the females who perched across the street. Some guys would stare out our classroom windows whenever the girls would venture into their playground wearing their oh so cute plaid skirts. The boys and girls were truly separated, no dances, no activities together except for, if my memory serves me right, our long awaited eighth grade Confirmation and Graduation.

We were thrilled to go on class trips, (boys only); we went to places such as Rye Beach, similar to Coney Island but in Westchester County, and to Washington DC, where we would stay in a fancy hotel, with three roommates. It was exciting being away with your peers, supervised somewhat but being allowed to grow up a little. I recalled having our entire group go to an automat for dinner one night. I believe it was Horn and Hardarts.' I remembered reaching in that special glass window and taking out the most delicious piece of southern fried chicken I had ever eaten! I wasn't hard to please. We also visited the White House and had our class picture taken on the steps of the Capitol with our Congressman. We were special!

*Time flew by and soon after we moved to the boys'
school it seemed like we were moving out. We would
have our class vote for most popular, best athlete, class
president, vice president, etc. I didn't win, don't know
if I even got a vote, (you weren't supposed to vote for
yourself, but we thought some kids did!). What started
out as a goofy prank became a nice badge of honor.
Some of the wise guys kids wanted to name Horace
Figorello, a kid who was quiet, as Class President.
Indeed he won and it drew a big laugh. I was friends
with Horace and would hang out with him. He was a
nice guy, quiet but funny in his own way. In the end,
however, Horace got the last laugh: he can always say
and prove that he was voted Class President!*

*We were being prepared to graduate as seasoned eighth
graders, about to venture onto the strange scary world
of high school. We were prepared for this milestone
thanks to the excellent work of our most dedicated
nuns, brothers and lay teachers. There were no
scandals, no crimes, no drugs, no PTA's, no anger and
no nasty made for TV scenes.*

*Just before our graduation however, one fine day in
May of 1963, our class made a vow to all get together
again in 25 years at the same spot to renew our
acquaintances. Someone did arrange this but it was 10
years later at our 35th. It was an amazing scene. It was
quite odd seeing how tall some of the boys got, how the
tall ones seemed to grow shorter, how some of the pretty
girls didn't seem quite as pretty anymore and how some
of the ones who weren't so pretty as kids, aged quite
well. Classmates who weren't really friends became*

friendly, at least for the evening, forgetting possible childhood social issues. The odd thing for me was some people whom I didn't recognize when I first became reacquainted with them, over the course of the evening their face would magically go back in time….that boyish / girlish face hidden beneath some wrinkled and sun drenched marks went away to make them appear to be 13 once again.

I am not sure if any friendships were renewed or commenced, but as for me, it was a very nice night. An enjoyable way to spend an evening, count my blessings due to the great path my life had taken and end it with memories refreshed but with no new beginnings.

Party Lines

Doctors wore beepers and perhaps lawyers too. Everyone else used either their home phone or a public phone. No mobile phones, no wireless access, no handhelds. Everything had to be hard wired to work. Most homes had one phone; it was a heavy black piece of equipment. They rarely if ever broke. They had what was called 'pulse' dialing with a rotary on it, which meant you needed your index finger or a good pencil eraser head to dial the round circle of numbers. Make a mistake and you had to redial, not by hitting a redial button but by actually redialing every single number. At least we didn't need to dial area codes, as all of Long Island was in the 212 area until they broke us into our own 516 section. Eventually everyone would place a phone on the wall in the kitchen and then the Princess phone came along which looked dandy in the master bedroom.

No one thought of owning a phone, they were leased from AT&T, aka Ma Bell. And even then many a family had a shared plan. A real share plan, with another family! We had party lines. You didn't know whom these people were who you shared your phone number with but if you picked up your phone and heard someone talking it was polite to hang up. It made for interesting conversation. We were thrilled when we finally got our own private line. We made it to the big time! Pioneer 2 – 6745.

The Gates had an exterior door leading out from their dining room to their backyard. It made them appear to be rich, as most others didn't have this odd feature, at least on our block. It was really cool; you could actually go into their backyard from their dining room. It therefore meant they had three exterior doors rather than the two that everyone else had.

Eventually, years later, Mom had a carpenter put one in our home too, which eliminated my little vegetable garden, whose main purpose seemed to be to feed some rabbits my home grown lettuce! The Gates' door also gave them a direct view of their garage. I don't recall them ever putting a car in their garage; it was more of a storage center. In fact, I don't think anyone put a car in their garage. They were used for supplies, much the same as sheds are used today. Our garage had tools, ladders, bikes, junk and oh so much stuff that Dad would save, collect and gather.

The Gates had tools too, and work benches and electrical contraptions that I had no clue what they were meant for. Mr. Gates was an electrician. He worked for years for a company called Jenney Electric, a local firm in Mineola. It also meant that he would do all our new electrical wiring and odd electrical repairing in our house, including setting up both the attic and basement when Dad physically and personally finished them to increase our living space.

But back to that dining room window. Scott and I were roughly the same age and we played together often. He was a grade ahead of me and roughly some 10 months older. Scott wasn't really into sports, he would rather delve more into building things and playing adventure games, such as soldiers, hunting, hide and seek, superheroes, etc. Adam, his younger brother, was really into sports, I mean obsessed. He could cite players, rules, and statistics even when he was in the playpen! Years later, Adam and I grew very close and played our own brand of baseball in both his driveway and on the corner of Macrame and Memory. For years we would do our own special game until my back surgery put me on the disabled list. I assumed that Adam stopped playing the game as well. Perhaps he claimed a new player on waivers.

One summer day, when we were about eight, Scott and I decided we would be cowboys. We were to be the good guys and Adam would be some sort of movie made bad guy. So we 'captured him' and decided he would have to pay the penalty that the cowboys supposedly gave the Indians -> a hanging. Hey, true to the silver screen, our plan was to devise a <u>fake</u> hanging. At least we didn't attempt to do what we thought the Indians actually did to the Cowboys: a scalping!

We didn't have any intent to harm Adam, only to enact what seemed to be some really cool and totally harmless childhood fun. So we contrapted some sort of mechanism in the Gates' garage by using the heavy wooden beams that ran across the top of their open garage door. The plan was that Scott would get a noose, put it around Adam's neck and I would hold him up, to make sure he didn't actually choke, hang or get hurt. It was a masterful foolproof plan.

Unfortunately, we had a wee little bit of a problem. Somehow, the box that we had Adam stand on wasn't quite strong enough to hold him. It quickly gave out but I courageously grabbed him, to protect him from the ultimate danger. I held him tight as could be as Scott and I worked feverishly and successfully in our attempts to take the noose off. So, in a roundabout way, you might say, we were actually heroes. Indeed, for we truly saved Adam's life! Thank you!

What one sees with one's eyes isn't always the truth. Perception is not always reality. Remember that dining room door that looked out onto the Gates' backyard? Well as luck would have it, Mrs. Gates just happened to be passing by her dining room when she took a quick glance outside to check on us kids playing and saw her 'baby' Adam dangling from a noose around his neck with me holding him.

While she didn't know if I was raising him or lowering him, she did see danger! Out the door she flew, into the garage she ran. By then, we had Adam safely on the ground and thought we did a fine job in cleaning up the mess. We were looking for some sort of praise and recognition. She angrily thought otherwise.

Scott and I were scolded pretty badly. Then the worse that could be happened.

Mrs. Gates proceeded to march me to our house. She went to our side door, rang the bell and Mom came out. It wasn't like the Burkes where she could just knock and walk in, even though they were cousins; it was still a little bit different. Mrs. Gates started telling Mom the story about how I had tried to hang her Adam. For whatever reason, Scott's participation in the whole scheme wasn't even mentioned. I tried to defend myself, but Mrs. Gates became both the Judge and Jury in this closed case of juvenile justice. Mom had a look in her eye; you know that look, the one that says: 'trouble is a brewing.' Mom had an uncanny ability to 'throw a look' – a glance from her eye; she could throw it across a room, across a hall, across a baseball field, and when you saw it, or when you caught it, because we would try to avoid it, you knew you were in trouble. That afternoon, I got the eye! Oh yeah, I got the eye!

So I knew then that I was going to get it from both sides. After stating her case, Mrs. Gates firmly announced her sentence: Judge Gates ruled: I was forbidden to enter their backyard for a period of <u>one year</u>!

Gosh, a whole year! That was like 1/8th of my lifetime! Mrs. Gates left and I explained to Mom what really happened. Mom didn't do any further punishment to me, Mrs. Gates was deemed quite enough, but it was tough. And while she tried, Mom couldn't get me a reprieve from the judge!

The months would go by and Scott and I would plan how much longer it would be for me to once again enter their property. Near the end, we counted the days until my sentence would be up. When that day finally came, it was like I was getting a pardon from the Governor! – I was a free man again! I could walk tall and not have to peer over the fence into their backyard at the other kids from the block!

I did indeed however love Mrs. Gates – and grew very fond of her for years afterward. I became really close to Adam a few years later as we played our endless games of both Gates' driveway and Maximus Place corner street baseball. But that was one very tough sentence that she handed out, a very long term and I really believed I was innocent. I always appreciated the fact that Mom and Dad believed I was as well.

Their faith in Jerry and me waned a little bit that same summer when Mom and Dad went out for a Saturday evening. Dick, who was 15, was also out, Jerry, who was 12 and me, a bright nine year old, were told to watch our baby sister Deb. She was three. Deb was put to bed, Jerry and I watched TV. At our appointed bed time, uh, yeah right!, Jerry and I went to bed. Our room was in the attic, somewhat removed from civilization below us.

Around 1 A.M., Mom and Dad were not yet home but supposedly Dick was. He was asleep in his room. Deb woke up and went into Mom and Dad's room, didn't see them; didn't think of venturing up another flight to look for us, instead she went downstairs and found no one there. Dressed in her charming tiger pajamas, with her feet wrapped in tiger paws, she decided to go find our parents. So to the front door she went, opened it and started walking down the block. Luckily, the Gates were arriving home at this time and as they pulled into their driveway they encountered our baby sister walking aimlessly into the night.

Mrs. Gates jumped out of the car and went over to Deb to ask her what she was doing. Somewhat startled, Deb said she was looking for her Mommy and Daddy. Into our house they both came, Mrs. Gates checked all of our bedrooms to find us all snuggled under our covers and then waited downstairs for Mom and Dad to arrive a few minutes later, since they were all at the same gathering.

Let's just say, we had a lot of 'splainin to do' the next morning, and we didn't watch Deb for a long time after that!

Dick, Cars, Airplane Trips, Parties and ... Mrs. Gates

Dick, as our eldest broke the ground for Jerry, Deb and me. He really did an excellent job at it. Simply said, he liked to see how far rules could be stretched before there would be any repercussions. He also liked new challenges, opportunities, excitement and ...well ok, parties and girls!

__Challenges__ – One day while in high school, Dick decided he wanted to fly in an airplane. Except for Estelle, no one in the family ever flew anywhere! But Dick had this bug about seeing what it would be like to fly. So one particularly quiet day after school, he sees an ad in the paper for a round trip ticket from New

York's LaGuardia Airport to Philadelphia. (In case you were not aware, JFK was called Idlewild back then and it was not the mega airport it is today). The price was a low, low total of $28.00. So Dick had a plan: that morning he would leave home, walk to his bus stop to go to school, but on the way to the school bus, he would turn left instead of right, and head directly to the New York City bus, take it a number of stops to the 179th Street subway and then maneuver his way to LaGuardia. His timing was flawless. His plan was masterful. His creativity was unique. His knowledge of school rules and their process, however, wasn't quite as good!

He figured that he would arrive home the same time his school bus returned. Mom and Dad would be none the wiser and he would have one more story to add to his mental mantle, which by this time was growing quite large. He had only one problem, he forgot to have someone notify his high school that he would not be in class that day. When he returned home, in full uniform, he proudly tried to walk in the side door, which was the door we always used. However before he got there, Mom and Dad were standing at the front door waiting for him.

Supposedly the dialogue went something like this:

Dad: So, where were you today?

Dick: Uh, school, where else would I go?

Mom: Well we received a phone call today saying you

never made it to school and we were worried sick about you. (Normally Mom would iron whenever Dick was out late, worrying sick about his whereabouts, but we don't know if ironing was also a daytime worry chore, so she probably rearranged the furniture instead)

Dick: Oh, shoot, Oh, gee, well, ok, I went to Philadelphia.

Dad: YOU WENT WHERE?

Dick: Philadelphia, I always wanted to go there.

Mom: Ok and how did you get there – walk?

Dick, No I bought an airline ticket for $28.00, here it is.

We don't know if Dick was punished for that one or perhaps rewarded for getting such a great deal! A $28 roundtrip ticket to Philadelphia! Amazing!

***Opportunities** – A few years later, while I was a freshman in high school, I came home and saw this gorgeous brand new Olds Cutlass sitting in front of our home. It was green with white trim and had beautiful white leather seats. It was a stunning car. Gosh, we must have some fancy company I thought. At about the same time Dad came home from work and asked Mom whose car was front of our house? Dick answered the question by advising that it was indeed his. Dad, who by this time didn't know what to believe, asked again. Dick told him that he went with a friend to the local Olds dealership. They had a tremendous sale which* *required very little down payment and because he was 21, he could legally buy the car. I thought it was just great. Dick could drive me to sports practices and all the other kids would look at the new wheels. It was impressive to say the least. Unfortunately, Dick was drafted into the Army a few months later and decided to sell the car rather than make the payments and not be able to use it. So the three of them worked together to try and sell his car, which they finally did: to the parents of a former kid in my class. Perhaps they also saw how cool it was when we pulled up for practice! Such a bummer for me!*

Excitement – *Dick would often go out with his friends in the evening. If he was out late, Mom would stay up anxiously awaiting his return. If it was real late, she would get up out of bed and start ironing to stay busy. I recalled one particular evening, while I was lying in the hospital bed due to my back surgery, Dick was out real late. If you recall, there were no cell phones or beepers, so it was very hard to get in touch with someone in an emergency. At three A.M, all of a sudden a police car pulls up in front of the house. Mom freaked out, thinking the worst. With that, Dick gets out of the car, says a few words to the police officer, closes the door and heads towards our house. When he gets in, Mom is hyperventilating. She asked Dick what that was all about. He responds that while he was at a bar, a cop was there and they got to talking, Dick needed a ride home, and the cop offered to drive him on the way back to his precinct.*

Because of Mom's never ending ironing and Dick's late

night adventures, our clothes were always neatly pressed!

Parties – *One hot summer week, our family had plans to go upstate to a resort for vacation. We were all going to go, except for Dick who asked if he could stay home and work. After all, he was older, and could fend for himself. Mom and Dad talked through it and finally agreed to let Dick stay home. The week went well, we all had a great time and we figured Dick did as well. Turned out, his week was better than ours!*

Dick, working with his friends from high school and from the neighborhood planned a really cool house party. They implemented very strict rules and a lot of teenage prep work went into their corporate strategy for the event. They had a pre-party meeting at our house. It was decided then that they would take the living room couches and place them on the stairs so no wild eyed teenage couple could venture off into an upstairs bedroom. The plan worked. No one went upstairs. The core team included Dick's good friend Cary, who also helped with the hiring of bouncers from the local public high school football team. They were there to prevent any outsiders (ruffians?) from trying to make entry into our house.

Somehow, one of the friends got their hands on Deb's life sized Raggedy Ann doll. He went into the front of our living room, near the window and pretended to have a wild make out session with the doll. All the kids laughed and enjoyed the escapade. The only problem was the blinds were open and Mrs. Gates had a clear eyed view of the scene. When we returned home from vacation on Saturday morning, we no sooner pulled into the driveway when Mrs. Gates came bolting out of her front door to our car to give Mom and Dad her report, which of course included the hot make out session that she witnessed through her window. Let's just say that Mom and Dad had a chat with Dick!

Girls – *While Dick was our family ladies man, his Army career brought him to Cleveland. It was there that Dick luckily found his Diane, who has truly been his most lucky charm, trusted partner and the true love of his life.*

Diane certainly tamed the Tiger!

Mr. Gates had a few things about him that we vividly recalled – he was short, he was loud and you really didn't want to get him angry. In the very beginning of this journey we were greeted with his most famous incredibly loud call of **'ADDDDDAAAAAAAMM!!!!'** He had such a booming voice for a slight man.

I remembered Mom telling me the story as I lay in my home hospital bed of what happened when Chad was born. Mr. Gates had grey hair, so he may have looked a little older than his years. Upon Chad's birth, supposedly the nurse walked into the expectant Dads' waiting room and happily announced to Mr. Gates that he had a 'Grandson.' Proud parental joy and a punch to the gut in one fell swoop! Mr. Gates was extremely dedicated to his kids. As was Mrs. Gates! He would stand by his kids through thick and thin. I remembered how touched I was when, as a teenager; Mr. Gates came out of his house with a brand new baseball glove that his boys had given him for a birthday present. It was the exact same model I had! He would have catches with all of us. When we compared gloves, we bonded. A very different personality when he came to play ball with the neighborhood kids. He loved to play catch.

Mr. Gates would really get excited when you talked about the Mets – a team he liked, along with his son Kyle. Scott didn't really show a favorite team, but Adam was a diehard Yankee fan. We would debate endlessly about whose team was better, and back then, my Mets didn't stand a chance! I would have been thrilled if we could only have had one player who could even make their lineup! 1969 for me and my Mets was still years away and no one ever saw it coming in the early 60's.

While Mr. Gates had a booming voice he also had a fearless and quite fearful dog named Franz. Franz was a larger than life German Shepherd. He looked like 'Rin Tin Tin,' but had a personality of a Fort Knox Watchdog. You had to make sure that you entered their house with one of the members of the Gates family or Franz would not be happy. No one wanted to learn what the alternative might lead to!

Not that Franz would bite you, but he could bark and growl with the best of them. I remembered someone taught Franz the words "Sic em" meaning 'to bite.' Once some kid, I don't recall whom, but legend had it he was from another block, came running after one of the Gates' boys. Franz saw this from behind his front screened door – from where he would sit as he overlooked and held court controlling his neighborhood day after day. When the 'chase' came into Franz's line of vision, hearing or smell, he broke out of the house and started a chase of his own - after the kid. None of us ever wanted to experience that. Ironically, no one ever found out what happened to the kid. Franz eventually came home. He seemed quite happy.

Once you were in the house with one of the Gates' kids, Franz was an entirely different dog. Peaceful, calm and loving, he was actually a great pet while always having the character of being the epitome of a vigilant watchdog.

In their defense, the Gates had a real reason for a

guard dog.   One night, while the family was sleeping, an intruder broke into their quiet house, walked up the stairs, entered their master bedroom and proceeded to take Mr. Gates' wallet from his dresser bureau along with other valuables … as they slept! It was a story that went through our very peaceful neighborhood.   The Gates were asleep and a burglar was in their bedroom! We didn't have crime issues on Memory Lane!   There was no such thing as house alarms, so people only had two other options, only one of which was considered viable. No not guns, no one – at least no one we knew of, had a gun in their home.   No one could blame them for   getting Franz after that!

Our thoughts then shifted to Thanksgiving, our Family Feast and Kyle. Starting in the years we were 'grown up' college age kids, Kyle would visit our home during dessert.   It was always very genuine and we would gauge when he would make his entrance. It was a really special moment and we all enjoyed it, especially Mom. Over the course of time, various members of the Gates' clan, extended family, grandchildren, etc. would come over, but the one constant was always Kyle, until he moved away to the Mid West ending a cherished holiday tradition which included the rewinding of old memories, the making of new ones and our never ending hot stove discussions about our shared favorite team: The Mets!

Childhood Fear

I only recalled being lost twice, once in First Grade I took the wrong bus home and went all over town, upset and nervous, but was thrilled when I saw my Dad and my brothers in our car on Hillside Avenue looking for me! Maybe that's when Mrs. Gates started driving us! The other time Dad took us boys to New York City to try and find hidden money from Bill Cullen's morning radio show in Grand Central Station. Dick almost found it, but his hand didn't go all the way to the back of a phone booth where it was indeed found. Stupid me, however, turned the wrong way and saw nothing but strangers. What felt like hours, was really a minute, but I learned to stay real close to my family after that!

While the Gates taught me the meaning of Discipline they also taught me the meaning of Appreciation, for all we shared for many years.

Dad, Mom and their dear friend Marjorie Emken celebrating life

THE SEMELRATHS

We next made our way some 25 feet to the left and found ourselves in front of the Semelrath house. We recalled, in our early years, another family lived there, but our memories of them were faded. Perhaps as this spreads again to my siblings, it will rekindle those forgotten cells. But we remembered the Semelraths, who in many ways were a most interesting group of people.

They moved to our block with two sons – Flint and Curt. Flint liked lizards, animals, all sorts of creatures. He was really into it. He was also fast, extremely fast – he could run with the very best of them, which meant he could take on either Dennis or Paul Burke to see who the fastest runner on our block was! A most distinguished and mighty recognition to be held in the highest esteem indeed!

Curt, the younger brother, didn't seem to possess the scientific inklings of Flint, but he did come across as a bit more athletic in sports other than track and field.

Both Flint and Curt had vibrant fire engine red hair, as did their younger siblings Susan and Matthew, who were born while they lived in the house. We forgot much about them except for the memories of them standing in a playpen in their side yard, next to the Gates' driveway. Back in the 50's - 60's there was no fear of kidnappings, child molesters or any other deviant behavior. It was sort of like Pollyanna became everyone's neighbor. That was why, when the Semelraths kept their young daughter and son in the fencing by their side yard, it made many of the other kids on the block look upon this with awe. We knew of pets that were held behind fences, but never a child. The Semelraths indeed were ahead of the times!

Housed in a wiry frame, Flint later became what one now might now call a computer genius. He was surely our block's Steve Jobs. I spoke with my siblings about how years after our youth, in the 1980's when Commodore Computers were first getting started, I would run into Flint in weekly meetings at our local library, which I attended with my good friend John, in order to expand our much needed computer literacy.

Johnny and I thought we were ahead of our times, as owners of our new Commodore 64's and 128D's! But when we went to these meetings, we were surely outmatched. These were meant to be PC educational sessions, but at times, in the back corner of the room, stood a few true computer literates exchanging software years before the internet had them do it in the safety of their own homes. By our attending these sessions, in no way did it verify that Johnny nor I deserved nor sought a title of computer geek nor did we participate in these activities! We were merely innocent observers who wouldn't know what to do with anything anyone could have given us. We were merely there to be educated and informed computer users. We were there to learn the basics!

As for Curt, well, we never knew what happened to him or his sister and brother. We didn't really know their parents that well. They sort of kept to themselves and we weren't sure if they mingled with the other parents. Our recollections of them were somewhat weak. We did, however, recall one particular rainy night. This was the day the Semelraths sadly produced one of the most frightening memories of all on our block.

Their dad, who was a nice man, was working a night shift for a company in Western Long Island. I thought it was in Elmont. I recalled it was a night which had terrible weather. Word spread in the morning about a car accident. Quickly when the news went around the neighborhood, it was not good. Their dad, Mr. Semelrath was killed. It was such a sad time. Neighbors visiting them; talking to them; hugging them; full food trays entering their home; empty ones leaving it. There was a constant stream that week. All of the attention one never wants to receive as participating residents of a block, they suddenly had to absorb in one enormous giving of love and care.

A few years later Flint married a local gal. They bought their childhood house from his Mom. He then brought his bride to live in the house that he grew up in and thereby made it into their new home. We knew by now, that houses were mere buildings, physical structures; and the people who lived in them were what converted these houses into a home. Flint therefore had two distinctive homes in the same house. By doing so, he became the new Mr. Semelrath on our block. Both through our computer club and the fact that Flint's wife ended up working in the high school where I live, we kept somewhat in touch. That is until they suddenly decided to move and ended up heading out west, never to be heard from again. They were nice people.

The Semelraths taught me Vision. They were truly ahead of the curve. We then walked to the corner house…..

THE GOLDENS

Walk we did, about 30 more steps, to the corner house, on Memory Lane and Leo Place. The Goldens were quiet people. We didn't really know the father or even recall if we had ever met him, at least Deb and I didn't. We shared a belief that he had passed away years earlier, when we were all very young.

Mrs. Golden lived in this big brown brick house on the corner, with the big green bushes on the front left side – bushes that were perhaps if not the best, then the second best hiding places for hide and seek on the block. She shared the house with her son, Randy. Randy was a quiet kid, in age probably somewhere in between Jerry and me. But he didn't really seem to play with anyone. He was not involved, which was difficult for anyone back then. What was the problem? We could only recall a few times he actually participated in any of our block's children activities.

Heck, he may have even missed the Memory Lane 1960 Olympics! This was very odd, because our block had a great many things going on every day. Living there was like a never ending circus or a day camp for kids – all the time.

Dick recalled that the Goldens were the only non Catholic / Christian family on our block. We didn't know what that meant at the time of our growing up, wasn't everyone Catholic? Was that why the Goldens moved?

Race, Religion and Politics

Back then we didn't know that there were many different religions. We thought of it simply as follows: Catholic, Protestant and Jewish.

For no real reason, other religions didn't really enter our conversations or life back then. We did study in school about Muslims and learned they originated in the Mid-East and were founded by a great prophet named Mohammed. We understood that the three great religions all had roots in the same area of the world, near where Adam and Eve started it all. Our little knowledge of Mormons was via the TV evangelist Oral Roberts who, as we witnessed on the tube, would put his hands on someone's head and heal them. We also thought Mormon men had a lot of wives.

The Protestants, as we later found out, were divided into many other factions, Episcopalian, Lutheran, Methodist, Baptist, etc. But to us kids, someone was either Jewish, a Protestant or Catholic. The Goldens were our Jewish neighbors and the Garretts down the block were the Protestant neighbors. Talk about us being sheltered!

During summer school, which was a series of summer fun programs based on sports and creative adventures rather than being remedial courses, we discovered that there were blacks in our village. No one heard of the terms Caucasian or African Americans; it was either white or black. The black kids were very nice and every year we would intermingle and play with them during our much anticipated fun filled program run by Mom and Dad's friend and local politician, Mr. Robin.

We didn't know where the black kids went to school during the regular school year because oddly we didn't see them during other times of the year. None of us ever thought of race as being an issue. Truth be told, the way we kids saw society really showed the way all adults should have lived in society. We saw no difference in the color of one's skin.

Except for President Kennedy's election, we never thought about religion, race or any of that stuff. There was never any prejudice in our home. There never was any negative talk about Blacks, Hispanics, Asians, Italians, Polish, Jews, etc. We honestly and quite fortunately grew up in a home where everyone was equal. I never heard a racial or religiously slanderous statement from either Mom or Dad.

We were thrilled when President Kennedy ran for the oval office. Our block was tickled pink. He was Catholic! The kids figured we would do our part and campaign for him so we rode our bikes to the local JFK / LBJ Campaign office and got our hands on all sorts of signs. On election day, with school being closed, so many of the younger kids on the block decided to ride our bicycles throughout town with our homemade placards which had JFK's picture on them. It was quite an impressive parade. About 15 of us rode all through the village. However, our enthusiasm almost met with incredible disaster.

We rode to the edge of town where the train tracks magically separated the rich folk of East Williston from the regular folk of Williston Park. We were the regular folk. Perhaps rich in the mind, but not in the bank.

None of us knew much about trains, electricity, tracks or something called the third rail. We only knew that the third rail meant danger but we didn't know from which way one counted to get to the third rail. Was it the third from the right or third from the left?

We parked our bikes and decided to take a well deserved rest on the tracks and eat our lunch.

We saw that one track was covered with this very long thick piece of wood. It was a perfect place to sit and enjoy a long awaited meal. So all of us stupidly sat down on the wood covering the actual third rail and dangled our feet below it while eating our lunch.

Miraculously, nothing happened. In fact we never even knew we were in danger until later that day when one of the kids told their parents where we went and what we had done. Phones rang, kids were summoned, lectures given and we were scared for life due to how close we all came to a frying on the tracks!

The only racial comment I could recall was one which was really a product of Dad's sense of innocent humor. He liked corny jokes and would come out with them whenever he felt the moment needed it.

I remembered one day, when I was around seven, driving in the car by the City Line on Hillside Avenue. I asked Dad why some people were black and others were white. He thought for a while and then said, 'it's simple, white people are born during the day and black people are born at night.' I thought to myself, hmm, I was born at 8:20 P.M., but it was in the summer so it was Daylight Savings Time…so maybe that's how it worked!

Later on, I obviously learned that that was not true. I also knew that Dad did not speak it in a hateful way. That was not Dad nor Mom's manner, method or belief.

We were raised to be strong Catholics. It was a most fundamental part of our upbringing. Confession was always on Saturdays, and Mass and Holy Communion were on Sundays. Dad, with his work schedule, could not always attend Mass on Sundays and back then, Masses were only on Sunday mornings. He would attend Mass on his own on Saturday's or weekdays to make up for it. Guess he was ahead of the times because once Saturday evening Masses were approved, he was golden.

I remembered sitting next to him on the days when we did attend Mass together on Sunday. I would always hold the Prayer Missalette up high, so Dad could follow along. Why he never held it on his own, I never knew or questioned; I often thought, without his glasses, he couldn't read the print anyway. But after a while, it became my pleasure to be the one to hold the book for Dad during Mass. While Dad could certainly hold it himself, in an odd way, I believed that he appreciated this tiny act of kindness.

In the evening, on my way to bed, I remembered walking past Mom and Dad's bedroom, usually after Dad went up because he had to leave for work very early in the morning. At times, I would peer through his slightly opened door and see my Dad kneeling at the side of his bed, head in his hands, saying his evening prayers. This is a most touching memory of my Dad.

We would say Grace before meals, especially on Sundays and Holidays such as Thanksgiving and Christmas; we prayed the rosary as a family in the evenings of May; we proudly exhibited our large Family Bible and had our house and garden statues blessed by the parish priests; and once in a while we even had Mass celebrated in our living room.

The four of us were thankful for the values that Mom and Dad gave us and our strong faith stays with us today. I recalled the day that I became an altar boy, it was in St. Aidan's auditorium for a Sunday Mass and I was serving along with my two older brothers. I was thrilled that we did it together! Unfortunately Deb could not share in that joy as girls, at that time, were not yet permitted to be altar servers.

Becoming a Eucharist Minister, as I moved on in years, is an honor that I truly appreciate and respect. To this day, whenever the priest raises the Host as he transforms the bread into the Body of Christ, I reflect back and silently thank Mom and Dad for the strong faith they instilled and fostered in us.

At some time in our life's passage through our block, the Goldens moved. I had thought it was after we grew up and moved on. Dick thought it was during our four life spans there. Whatever it was, one thing was very certain, the new people who moved in were Irish. A lovely young couple who came right over from Ireland moved in. You know what that meant – Mom made her way to their house to meet, greet and become friends with them. Another ally in green!

Mom truly did become a good friend with the lady of the house. They had no children. One day, while returning from work in New York City, her young husband took his nightly walk from the 179th Street Subway Station in Queens to his parked car in Jamaica. While walking, he met upon some thugs who robbed him and took more than his money. He was found in his car the next morning parked on the side streets of Queens. He was dead. A young man tragically left behind a very young widow.

Mom spent a great amount of time at their home consoling her friend. Years later, the favors were returned when Dad, who by this time was in a nursing home and Mom, while possessing a license, but didn't really drive, was always in pursuit of capable and enabled drivers. So her Irish friend became one of Mom's many drivers to church and Dad's nursing home. Eventually, her friend rebuilt her life, moved on, up and away from Memory Lane. Mom and she kept in touch via phone, because Mom wouldn't drive there. Notice I did not say Mom couldn't drive, because she surely could.

Driving

Mom did indeed pass her driver's test. She was quite proud of that, even though it took her three attempts to finally succeed. Knowing that Dad was becoming engulfed with Alzheimer's, she realized she would eventually need to someday take over the wheel. This in itself would become a real issue since Dad always did all of the driving. We all worried about Dad driving in his early stages of the disease. He would drive to Corona to visit his sister Carrie on Fridays. Supposedly he needed to go shopping for her. This seemed quite nice and loving, until one day he told Mom: 'I just don't know what happened, but I got lost driving home from Carrie's. This was a route he had taken for more than 35 years and her house was the house he grew up in. The signs of his illness were growing.

We tried so hard to have him stop driving. Every Thursday he insisted that he had to go to the local Grand Union to help the truckers deliver the weekly advertising circulars. He was so serious about this and felt that he would let them down if he didn't show up to help. In reality, it was a combination of Dad's very strong work ethic running into an unreal commitment due to Alzheimer's. But this weekly chore became the real impetus that helped us to finally have Dad stop driving.

One day my friend Ken's mom saw Dad driving the wrong way on a major road by our house as he came out of the shopping center. In the end, we had to 'lose' Dad's keys to get him to stop. So a few days later, I basically took his keys and lied to him saying that we couldn't find them. Together we would look and look, with all sorts of strange disloyal feelings going through our minds. This was our Dad and we were now treating him like a child, but we knew we had to have him stop driving before he would hurt himself or God forbid someone else. Over the course of only a few weeks, it worked and miraculously Dad stopped looking for his keys! His Alzheimer's was truly getting worse and he simply forgot about it; at least that is what we all told each other.

As Mom was starting to drive, she accidently slid her car on some wet leaves, ironically right next door to our Uncle John's home, which was around the corner from ours. Her car went onto the curb and just missed a tree. It caused Mom to basically shut down her driving career, though I kidded her that she was a fully licensed excellent back seat driver! She didn't like that then, and surely not now. However, every three years, Mom would proudly renew her actual license – just in case it would be needed.

Me and Mom e 1988, most likely with a leprechaun on her lapel!

In our teens Dad was our official driving coach. Once with Jerry at the wheel, after he just received his license, the police pulled Jerry over. Dad didn't want Jerry to get into trouble, so in an age before seat belts, without hesitation Dad slid Jerry from the driver's seat, and as the officer approached the car, Dad was indeed the 'driver.' Dad then calmly explained his way out of the issue. Crafty but quite masterful!

When it became my turn, Dad's car was a Chevy Vega, with stick shift and I just couldn't get the handle of it. No pun intended. So I received special assistance from our Aunt Margie. Aunt Margie and Dad's youngest brother, our Uncle Johnny, lived around the block from us along with our cousins Barbara, Marjorie and Eleanor. Uncle Johnny was my Godfather and my personal favorite uncle. Up until his death at the age of 80, we had a special bond. Aunt Margie's white car was automatic, so I learned on that, many times with her sitting next to me. I passed on the first try! Aunt Margie was also very happy that I passed. She got her car back! I was thrilled too but had no car to drive!

That's me walking on Memory Lane e 1957

Curse Words, Not In Our House!

I must have been around seven years old, when as Dad drove Mom, baby Debbie and me home from some shopping in Mineola, we passed by a few factories. Being a newcomer to the world of reading, I carefully read the words written on the white exterior walls of the buildings. A few I would speak out loud. The car ride was quiet when I suddenly saw a word I didn't recognize. So I blurted it out loud: "Shit" I said.

Mom turned her head to me as quickly as I have ever

seen. *"What did you say?"* she said with firm parental passion. *I explained that I just read it on the wall and didn't know what it meant. Mom simply told me that I shouldn't say it again and then quickly changed the subject. Thinking back, though I never heard Dad ever say this word, he was probably getting a really big chuckle over this one!*

The Goldens taught me Meekness. As we approached Leo Place, we stopped walking....and looked towards our right....

LEO PLACE

We now crossed the street, looked to the right, down Leo Place, at a couple of homes that housed memorable families – first on the right, was the Boswells – Dick's good friend, Terry was their youngest. Dick had a lot of memories with Terry, but the one that stood out the most and stood the span of time wasn't about Terry but for his older sister, who for a brief period in the 50's supposedly dated a Yankee pitcher. That was like so cool! We tried to remember his name, for some reason, I thought it was some guy who came to the Yanks from the Dodgers in a big trade, but I could be wrong, it wouldn't be the first time!

Next to the Boswells was the Samson house. Not the guy from the Bible who got into it with David, but the Samsons.

They had a bunch of kids, one of them, named Chuck, who went to school with me, had a leg brace and was a bit on the wild side. I recalled him being one of the tough kids. Back then, the tough ones were called 'Hoods' and the good ones were called 'Sportrats.' We were Sportrats.

My most striking memory of the Samsons involved their Dad. The story went that one day Mr. Samson went to his doctor for some sort of check up. Later that day, he mysteriously and suddenly died at home. It was so eerie. The story spread throughout the neighborhood. I bet his doctor lost a lot of patients!

Down the block from them was a family that Jerry was close to, they knew him from his paper route, from church or just from being a kid in the neighborhood. They too would later become one of the many who would drive Mom to and from Mass.

Jerry and his followings:

For many reasons, Jerry seemed to always develop real bonds with a great number of our neighbors, many of whom were couples without children or couples who weren't truly a 'couple' as one would consider them. Jerry was the one among us who found neighbors that the rest of us didn't really know, such as the famous Mr. and Miss Boil.

They lived on Jerry's paper route. For years Jerry would do odd jobs for the Boils: mow their lawn, make minor repairs in their home, tend to their garden, shovel the snow, and clean their garage. Whatever and whenever they needed something done, for years, they would call Jerry. They paid him handsomely for these tasks in good old American greenbacks!

They also had a car that appeared to be one that Henry Ford worked on when he was a kid. It was old, but it worked and they and Jerry drove it. When Jerry did, it was sort of like Driving Miss Daisy New York style! Eventually, when their age caused them to cease driving, they either sold or gave it to Jerry and it became his first car. It was a tank, a large, grey heavy metal machine. It sat in our backyard for months until Mom and Dad finally let him use it. I remembered one day, while Jerry was away in college, Dad and I were in the backyard admiring Jerry's car and I got into the driver's seat. I turned the key, hit the gas and the car suddenly lurched forward. I had no idea what I was doing! Dad quickly ran to the driver's door, reached in to take control and the car stopped. Needless to say, I was not allowed in that car for quite a while!

When Jerry went off to college, for a short time, I replaced him as the Boil family designated Baumbach chore master, but they always seemed to like Jerry better than me. I would hear: 'Jerry did it this way, Jerry did it that way.' Geesh, what did he have on these people!

Interestingly enough, for years I thought this 'couple' was husband and wife, only to find out years later, they were actually a brother and sister sharing the same house.

Speaking of cleaning basements and garages, and the chores Jerry did, he truly did have a following. He became Aunt Mary's personal favorite to do her annual cleansing of her basement. We never quite knew where her 'stuff' would come from, living alone in her house, but wow could she collect and gather all sorts of things. Jerry was a master at getting rid of her old collectibles. Unfortunately this was years before Ebay, so her treasures went the way of the metal trash can.

Jerry's followers were much more than these folk. Many, many others in our village, our church and as you will soon see on our block were members of his personal flock. As his brother and also roommate for more than a decade, I proudly became one of them also and remain steadfastly so years later.

Spread out down Leo Place and across the street were the Gentrys and McAndrews of Great Products, where Mom had worked until I had my surgery. The two Gentry boys went to St. Mary's and were spaced in between Jerry and me. They were an interesting bunch. While not that involved in our Memory Lane antics, they became much more involved in our lives in later years.

Barry went to Marist College, was a Met fan and was a member of the class a year ahead of me, so we sort of stayed in touch, but it was with Dad that the connection was made, through their cocareers at Great Products Plumbing Supply.

Dad, his work and then some

Dad proudly worked for the A&P - Jane Parker Bakery for 34 years in Queens, NY. It was originally located in Maspeth and later moved to Flushing, right next to Shea Stadium, aka Citifield. Dad's former worksite is now a Home Depot, how times change!

When I needed a summer job in 1969, Dad secured me a position inside the bakery. Quite frankly I never saw anyone work faster or harder than Dad. He never ever stopped. I thought he was just that way at home, but I was wrong. Perhaps A&P Management thought I was the same way because of the manner I handled all of the boxes I had to keep unloading from a freight car at the bakery warehouse. But Dad, knowing the limitations of my back, protected me and had one of his supervisor pals give me a position unloading trainloads filled with cases and cases of – potato chips! From a distance, I looked like a weight lifter…I was good!

The daily grind of driving got to Dad and he retired at a relatively young age of 59. This retreat from work lasted about two weeks. Dad then went to Doubleday, the book company and landed a job working in their mailroom. Dad's brother-in-law, our Uncle Bill Shields, my second favorite uncle, had retired from being a mailman and worked in New York City in an ad agency's mail room and really enjoyed it. Dad figured he would too. He spent a week at Doubleday and clearly did not like the new adventure. Shockingly for all of us, he resigned, sending all sorts of messages to us. WHAT WAS GOING ON WITH OUR DAD!

Within a few weeks, Dad grew bored again. Through Mom's friendship with the McAndrew family, who owned Great Products, a rapidly expanding local plumbing supply company, she heard of an opening in their shipping department. Dad interviewed for the position, was hired and became an integral part of their 'family.' He absolutely loved the job and took his new responsibility extremely seriously, almost too seriously.

Dad had a passion for numbers. It became legendary in our family. He could add, multiply, subtract and divide faster than a computer. We would do tests – the calculator vs. Dad - and he would beat us 90% of the time. It was incredible. If you went shopping with Dad, which I did most every Friday afternoon after he came home from work, he would keep track of all of the items as the checkout guy / gal would tally the total.

This was always a large number, consisting of about 10 to 15 bags of groceries, and this was before the modern day cash registers. These were the old, black, big button ones that never showed the final amount until the end, and then only for the eyes of the checkout clerk. Well Dad would mentally check every item, keep a running total in his head, and at the conclusion, proceed to hand over the exact change. I will never forget the look on a new cashier's face as they would be handed the right amount. Years later, looking back, it is now personally regretful how this weekly venture, which took me away from my then valued playtime, can be so missed. Maybe that's why I am known to still get 'lost in the stores' when shopping with my family!

So it was therefore only natural that Dad would handle the shipping for Great Products and insure their on-time delivery by properly entering the zip codes for their many daily shipments. Nowadays, we have various on site shipping systems to help these transportation professionals, but back in the 60's and 70's, it was a manual process and one had to visually look up in a book the exact zip code for every destination. Dad would memorize them, all of them. Ironically, this became one of the first signs of Dad's Alzheimer's, which eventually did him in.

He would come home complaining about how loud his co-workers would talk in his shipping department. He claimed this chatter made it very difficult for him to concentrate and get his zip codes right. He was very frustrated by this, so much so that he went to his boss, who was also a friend, and asked to cut back on his hours, until eventually he couldn't handle the pressure and stress anymore and retired completely.

The McAndrews, and Dad's co-workers were great to our family and stayed close to Mom as Dad sadly mentally withered away. Checkers became his lasting passion. With his fingers severely weakened due to his illness, he painfully would reach for his checker pieces and move them ever so softly. He took on all challengers and while his mind seemed to be so very far away, his skill for playing checkers never waned. He always won. He really did!

As we finished our look down Leo Place, the last house we saw was the Heise Home. We had very few memories of these people.

I did remember that they had a tall blond son named Fritz, who occasionally played with us but was not really part of our Memory Lane collection of kids. Far more importantly, they owned an aromatic bakery in town, which we would visit with Dad on Saturday mornings. Hey, with a German name like Heise, it had to be good and when all was said and done our family truly loved bakery products! Just ask Jerry!

Dick and I playing Dad's favorite board game, Dick wouldn't let me win!

The McAndrews taught me Empathy, they understood, helped and loved Mom and Dad. We crossed the street and walked on...

THE QUICKS

We now walked across the street to the Quick house. It was the nice house on the corner with the cool bushes in the backyard that bordered the Heise home. These bushes were truly phenomenal hiding places, especially when we played Fox and Hound. Once I used these bushes to hide because I was a hound, it was so good and I was so remarkably quiet, that I stayed there for a long time and no one found me. I waited and waited....after a while I started to get a little concerned over this. After all, I was an okay player, but never a champion in the art of Fox and Hound Lore. So, I finally came out of my space, went looking for all the other kids and found that they had already started to play a totally new and different game. They all thought I went home. I never liked that Fox and Hound game after that.

The Quicks had a daughter named Paula who went to school with Dick. They were block and school friends, nothing more than that. Paula, while a good friend of Dick's, wasn't really his romantic type. As mentioned, Dick was our crooner, our Dean Martin, our Elvis, our James Dean, and our Brad Pitt. He sort of liked to party and liked the ladies, and the ladies seemed to like him. Mom seemed to be always cooking up dinner for another one of Dick's girlfriends. His black book could have been our door stop on windy days.

Mr. Quick was interesting. As kids, we never really knew what it was, but he talked with an odd voice, only later did we understand that he actually had a hole in his throat. Obviously something was wrong, but it was never talked about and he seemed to live a good long life. Years later, I had heard that Mom's brother, our other Uncle John, (we have three of them), after enduring the thrashes of polio, which eventually led to his demise, also had a tracheotomy. It was too big a word for us kids, a hole in the throat made far more sense!

WHY DIDN'T ANYONE TELL ME MY UNCLE JOHN DIED?

While I was away for many months recovering in the hospital from my spinal surgery, Uncle John passed away in his then hometown of Cincinnati. But I didn't know it for months. Mom and Dad didn't want me to know, afraid that it would affect my healing process as I was in between two major surgeries and was recovering from a serious staph infection which placed me in isolation. So for months, it was a secret. I did recall a few days when they couldn't visit me, but thought it was due to one of them being sick. Instead, they, along with Estelle, flew to Ohio for Uncle John's funeral.

Months later, while watching me, Dick told me what had happened and I thought he was nuts. Only when he showed me the press clippings about Uncle John's funeral did I believe him. I was ticked and only after a long talk with my parents did I understand why I was kept in the dark.

Uncle John was a cool guy who knew a lot of important and famous people. For years Mom would display a photo of him interviewing the famous heavy weight fighter Jack Dempsey. A few months after his death, I received a short but nice note from a Baseball Hall of Famer – Waite Hoyt, who was a teammate of Babe Ruth's from the 1927 Yankees. He said Uncle John asked him to write to me so that I would have a real connection to the Babe. Thanks Uncle John!

The Quicks taught me Compassion.

We marched, as a strong growing group, next door…

Note from Waite Hoyt from the 1927 Yankees - my link to Babe Ruth. He ends it by writing: 'If you see Yogi, tell him I said "Hello"!'

THE JITNERS

THE COLEMANS

Did you ever see a kid run out the front door of his house in his underwear? I always believed I did!

The story had legs, but supposedly Jimmy Jitner liked ice cream, so much so that one Sunday when the Bungalow Bar truck, (Good Humor and Mr. Softee hadn't come to us yet), came jingling down the street, Jimmy couldn't wait. Why he was in his underwear on a Sunday afternoon, we will never know, but all of a sudden this kid comes running out of his house chasing the ice cream treat truck down Memory Lane. Classic!

Jimmy would be between Jerry and Dick and quite frankly this is the only memory I have of him or his family.

Years after the Jitners moved; perhaps Jimmy's dad worked for Fruit of the Loom and was transferred to outerwear, a number of new families moved into the house. One was the Colemans, who, wouldn't you know, became another one of Mom's drivers.

The Colemans were nice folks, had a few young children and while none other than perhaps Deb knew much about them, at least they didn't run around the neighborhood in their skivvies!

For some reason, I believed Eric Coleman, besides being actively involved in Church activities, also became a political servant in the famous Taxpayers Party, which ran the town for eons. Our thoughts were that he never rose to mayoral status as the Fays and Kellehers did, but he was a Trustee which was a pretty prestigious level of local political accomplishment. One may say he was similar to a community organizer / activist.

The Jitners taught me Spontaneity! The Colemans taught me Involvement. And we walked a few steps to the left....

THE ROGERS

Heading east about 15 feet we found ourselves in front of the Rogers house. Another 'Williston Park Brother' from the Fire Department. In fact our block was full of local firemen – Dad, Artie Murray, Vincent Fay, Ted Howe, Tom Byrnes and Joe Rogers to name a few.

Mr. and Mrs. Rogers – Joe and Arleen as our parents called them, were in that sort of close second circle to our own primary inner circle on the block. They were lifelong friends and were active participants in the annual New Year's Eve Celebrations.

They both appeared to be younger than their years. With his blond crew cut haircut, Joe Rogers had the looks of a very much in shape ballplayer who was in the peak of his prime. His wife was similar. They had three children. Joe, the eldest, went through the early stages of his life being called JoJo by some of us on the block, which we all found out many years later was he was never really fond of this moniker. He was a few months older than me. He had a younger brother named Blake, who was a few years younger than me and a younger sister Sandy, who was closer in age to Deb.

All three of them took their Dad's blond looks. Their Mom was a brunette. Joe was the athlete. He could hit, run, field, do it all. An excellent hide and seeker, or whatever the activity, Joe was always in the top 10% of our block.

His brother Blake was a bit lankier and while a decent athlete didn't appear to be ranked in the same level / world class as his older brother. But things may have changed!

Their sister, Sandy, wasn't really involved with the boys, except when it came to playing kickball, she could really kick that ball! As she grew up, she grew into a very pretty blonde young lassie and no one really seemed to care anymore about her kickball skills.

The Rogers were another of the lucky ones on our block to have a pool in the backyard. Earlier we met the Howes who had a pool, but the Rogers had theirs' first. If you were lucky enough to be invited to a 'community swim' you were thrilled. The pool seemed so very deep, but was only about a foot and a half, but hey, it was wet and cold and on those hot, pre-air conditioner days, it served an incredibly welcome purpose.

We didn't know if Mrs. Rogers enjoyed her role of being the block lifeguard, or if in fact anyone did indeed enjoy playing that role. People for some odd reason didn't appear to have the same sense of caution around pools that we correctly have now.

Kids, Emotions and Tempers

At times in our lives most of us find ourselves embedded in various levels of society. It is similar to an informal 'caste system.' For many, it starts at a very young age and it occurs in various degrees. Occasionally on our block there would be an 'in' crowd. It would rotate depending on who was the best athlete or who had the best grades, or whoever possessed the current 'in' thing. It was not consistent and did not happen all the time. When you were 'in' you felt cool, when you were not, you felt lost.

The Rogers like all of us had a free standing garage for the storage of cars, bicycles, tools and lawn products. Besides the main garage door, they also had a separate glass paneled door. This entrance way would make it appear to become a club house of sorts, a place for occasional 'in' crowd meetings.

One summer day, I went to the garage and for some reason, I was not allowed in. It really annoyed me and I demanded to be permitted to enter. Kids being kids, they let me in, but then they all left and kept me in, locked inside.

I was frightened and wanted out. No one would let me leave, so I took matters into my own hands, literally and punched my right fist through the glass panel, broke it into pieces and unlatched the door. As I did this, I seared my thumb and the blood came pouring out. My temper got the best of me and foolishness overcame common sense.

Everyone freaked out with the blood as it was gushing out of my thumb. The Rogers now had a messy garage floor, driveway, and not to mention a broken panel of glass. And I had a throbbing bloody thumb. I ran home, where else, but to Mom. She did the nurse thing and somehow stopped the bleeding and bandaged it up for good. No one would think of going to the doctor or hospital for stitches. Later a small white scar formed on the inside of my right thumb that has lasted for years.

For whatever reason, this scar became my personal badge of courage. Over time, I knew that if I was ever in a tough spot, I looked at my thumb and somehow, someway, knew I would find a way out. It worked, especially as a teenager for the two years I spent in and out of the hospital recuperating from my back surgeries.

There was one other thing about the Rogers that was a bit different then the vast majority of our block. They weren't Catholic. They were Protestant.

As we aged and moved on, Arleen got ill and passed away, leaving their dad a relatively young widower.

JoJo, who by now was simply Joe, opened up a very successful house painting business in town. Thanks to Mom's never ending need to continually redecorate, she became a very steady customer. In fact, Jerry and Elaine also hired him to do their home as well...keeping it all in the family!

We lost touch with the rest of the family and never knew where they ended up or if indeed they still lived on our block as we stood in front of their house. We could have simply knocked on the door to see if they were still at home, but didn't.

The Rogers taught me Self-Reliance, we walked onto our left.

Me with hair, my bride Chris and Estelle e 1974

THE BYRNES

Can you imagine life without the internet?

What would life be like without Instant Messages, Facebook, MySpace, Twitter, cell phones? We knew because we lived it. Back then if news needed to travel, Jerry and I believed the messenger was right on our block, in the person of one Mrs. Byrnes!

Mr. and Mrs. Brandon Byrnes were a very nice couple with three kids. Two girls, Colleen, aged a year older than me, Megan, a year younger than me and Timmy, who was Deb's age.

Mr. Byrnes was a sprightly man. His wife had the charming look of Edith Bunker, complete with the apron, etc. Brandon Byrnes, as he was called, worked for or had a relationship with a meat company that sold pork butts.

Every once in a while, Mr. Byrnes would come to our house with a few pork butts, which Mom would cook as if they were corned beef. I often wondered why we would eat a pig butt, or why anyone would consider calling it that in the first place. But it tasted good and I never openly asked those questions, leaving it to my taste buds to decide rather than my mind.

I remember that many of the kids would want to play Spin the Bottle in the Byrnes' garage. I was kind of like, uh, what are the rules? and we have to kiss whom? Ugh. So I didn't play. I did remember watching one particular game where the bottle would go round and round and Scott Gates always seemed to be the winner.

As mentioned, when it came to communication, in the minds of Jerry and me, Mrs. Byrnes was the NY Times: all the news that can fit, she seemed to report. For whatever reason, we thought she had the inside track on anything happening on our block. Mom would tell us stories and we would say, where did you hear that from and usually the source would be 'from Mrs. Byrnes.' We wondered if she had both cub reporters and third party sources out there covering our street beat. She was a super nice lady who was our own Barbara Walters! Everyone liked her.

As the Byrnes were about to retire, they went into a business venture with the Rogers. The local pub around the corner was for sale and they decided to go ahead and buy it. It seemed fairly successful, enough that a few years later they sold it and then purchased a lodge in upstate New York, similar to a Bed & Breakfast with a restaurant on the premises, or so we were told! We visited once but then we all lost touch with them.

Games, Toys, Trains and Radios

The thrill of a new toy was nothing like the expectation of possibly receiving one. Kids of our era had to really work our parents hard to get a new toy or game. (Spin the Bottle being the obvious exception, as they supposedly didn't 'know' it was being played). As opposed to the modern day instant gratification syndrome that perhaps the children of the 50's and 60's created, our options were somewhat limited, but a great deal of fun nevertheless.

While we didn't have the TV or computer games of the current age, we did see the coming of the future with Jerry's cool electric football game which was basically a metal like surface that vibrated little metal players along an electronic field....humming all the way to the end zone. Most of the players kept falling down as the play ensued, which took a lot of time starting and stopping the plays over and over again as these guys stumbled their way to the end zone.

More tame toys were our green army soldiers, tiny in size but power packed in the emotion, they were truly a standard for most boys, as were the cowboy and Indian sets, with the little white railings and horse troughs – all about three inches by one inch but always ready to refresh a thirsty cowboy's horse with imaginary water. One of my personal favorites was a green metal car; it still lives, yet is a bit rusty due to the many days of being in the Murray's sandbox!

I also loved my two foot tall red robot, which had a special little door in his belly which I would fill with toast! I never knew why Robert the Robot thought he needed to eat toast, but I dutifully filled his belly with it. With fresh batteries, he could actually walk on my kitchen floor, not on the carpets though, since it would always cause him to go tumbling down!

I still have both my green car and my old pal Robert....both broken and tarnished but full of cherished memories of times long gone by.

The balls we used were multiple. We always used regulation sized footballs, no small things, except for the rare occasions when someone would get those really tiny footballs that we would be able to wrap our fingers around and throw perfect spirals. We rarely played tackle football, as two hand touch was the order of the day. Just in case though, we were always ready, with most of the boys having our own official football helmets (either NY Giants or Notre Dame logos) and shoulder pads. They were far more for show than substance.

Stickball was our beloved sport with that high bouncing

spaldeen pinkie! Barehanded, we could easily catch the ball, unless it was hit so hard that it would come popping out as soon as it hit our palm! When we played hardball, it remains a mystery how we could actually catch the ball, as our gloves were roughly half the size of what the kids use today. Many of my best games involved my standing in the outfield chewing on the leather cords that kept my glove intact. It was probably my own version of 'chew' or chewing tobacco, which the big leaguers used but has since been banned in many places. My chewing of leather was harmless for me but sadly not for the cow.

Besides playing actual baseball games at the Lots, we also enjoyed our hometown version of home run derby. Everyone wanted to be Mickey Mantle, Willie Mays or Duke Snider, which eventually led us to want to be Roger Maris. (Being New Yorkers, the Great Hank Aaron did not get the same attention). For the record, Harrison Howe was the only one to actually achieve the feat of hitting it over the fence, a mighty feat at that and it didn't have an asterisk attached to it!

One of my personal favorites was playing three flies / six grounders. That was always fun. And then there was the time I actually made three, yes three errors in one inning while playing second base, but then I got the next three outs to get us out of the inning unscored upon. Amazing irony! I turned those lemons into lemonade!

We would go to Kauder's Candy store and buy our nickel wax pack of Topp's baseball cards, which had the tremendous smell of pink bubble gum that was included in every pack. We would trade them or flip them (someone would normally call 'No Tips' meaning if the cards just barely touched, it didn't count and another round would be due). Perhaps our best use of our cards was to attach them to our bicycle spokes with a clothespin. We loved the motorcycle sounds they would make as we would cruise the neighborhood. The only cards that we craved for were once again those of Mickey Mantle, Willie Mays or Duke Snider. With Mantle's 1951 Topps card truly being the rarity.

If we only had a penny, we would gladly buy a piece of Bazooka bubble gum, which always had the cool little comic strip of Bazooka Joe wrapped around the pink square piece of gum.

Kickball, Punchball and Handball – which we were told by many that our Dad excelled at. There were tales of his stickball games and his two or three sewer home runs. Our block was never quiet. The girls on our block played some of the street ball games with us also, especially I Do So Declare, when we would throw the ball as high in the air as possible and call out someone's 'country.' If they caught it on a fly, the thrower was out, if not, they then had to throw it at someone else by declaring War on their Country.

When they weren't playing with us, the gals had their share of toys and dolls too. Betsy Wetsy who was born in the 1930's, saw a rebirth in the 50's then she suddenly appeared to have a fully developed older cousin when Barbie and some handsome dude named

Ken joined the scene, arriving together in her pink convertible.

Girls also had their pogo sticks; hopscotch chalk, which I confess, I also enjoyed, and jump ropes, which I never could master nor could I understand how they managed to do that Double Dutch rope thing! There were also the infamous Hula Hoops, which the girls seemed to be much better at than the boys. Had we been a little older we would have probably had more fun watching the girls do it rather than ever attempting to do it ourselves. I absolutely stunk at hula hoops! If it went around once, I was thrilled! I blamed my back!

Girls also had some sort of fashion board game with their special plastic outfits that would be rolled onto their little plastic models. I remember finding tons of these little pieces of Debbie's plastic clothing all over the house.

Debbie was especially good at Jacks, how she did it always amazed me. While we would all play pickup sticks, and roll our marbles all over the floor, I was told to use my toes to pick up my marbles so it would help with my pigeon toed feet. When we wanted some attention, we would start to have some fireworks with the rolls of caps that we could hit with a rock, watching the smoke as the crisp crackling sounds of mini explosions went off.

Board games were a major event, especially when it was a rainy summer day. Monopoly, Checkers, Clue, Scrabble, Go to the Head of the Class, Concentration,

Life (you had to love those little cars and the tiny, tiny families!), Risk, which I never understood, but would love to play now; Operation and Trouble, which was a Saturday night favorite we played with Estelle!

In the faraway places in the attic bedroom Jerry and I shared, I found a great place to hide some of my treasures, which meant a lot to me but most likely were useless to anyone else. For some odd reason, I went out of my way to collect Plaid Stamp books, not the actual Plaid stamps, which were similar to S&H Green Stamps which merchants gave out when you bought their products. I believe Plaid Stamps were given out at the A&P, which was a staple of shopping for our family, especially since Dad worked in their main bakery for 34 years. I would always bring home these books which had pages to place the Plaid Stamps on. Why I saved them, is now beyond my imagination. Certainly I believed these empty books would grow in value some day. Upon moving, I forgot to empty the drawer, which held the gray box hidden below our beds built into the wall. I trust the new owners have made a tidy profit thanks to my never ending efforts!

When the whistle blew in our basement, it meant that Dad set up our (his?) Lionel train set. This was so cool, with all the little shops and houses mixed in the village which had tracks circling them. We loved the opening and closing of the gates as well as the trainmen waving as the train came choo chooing along. The white smoke, which I had thought was caused by little white aspirin pills made it seem so realistic. There was always an internal battle over whose trains these were. Dick's or

Jerry's? No one seemed to include me or Deb in this debate. It quite peacefully came to an end some 35 years later when Jerry presented Dick with the big black locomotive, which Dick immediately added to his set, all reunited once again!

Me and My Dad e 1956

And if we had money to spend, there was a great choice between Skateland for ice skating, the Mineola Roller Skating Rink, the Mineola Movie Theater, McGuinness's amusement park and restaurant or the miniature golf park across the street located right next door to the Howard Johnson's restaurant with their great hot dogs and 28 tremendous flavors of ice cream!

I loved it when I was given my very own transistor radio, a little gadget that could slip under my pillow at night and get both music from Buffalo, NY and baseball games from St. Louis or Cincinnati. When my Mets had an off day, I enjoyed Harry Caray doing Cardinal games or Waite Hoyt doing the Reds games. In the late evening, if we couldn't sleep, we could listen to Long John Nebel and his unique guests. In the morning,

Mom always listened to Bill Cullen on 660 WNBC, until Herb Oscar Anderson (HOA) took over our home from the studios of 77 WABC and his fellow oh so cool DJ's: Dan Ingram, Scott Muni, Charlie Greer, Harry Harrison, Ron Lundy, Chuck Leonard, and "Cousin Brucie" Bruce Morrow. We also tuned into the WMCA Good Guys or Murray the K and The Swingin' Soiree on 1010 WINS. During the day, we were fascinated by the sports knowledge of Bill Mazur, and Mom was mesmerized by the one and only Bernard C. Meltzer as he opened his show with: "What's your problem?" As Mom would prepare dinner, we would sit down to a quick review of the day's news through the golden voices of two people: Alex Dreier's and 'Hello America' with Paul Harvey.

The Byrnes taught me the power of Communication. We then gathered our thoughts as we were about to go a house we never knew....

Dad, his buddies and his younger brother Johnny.
Dad is second from top left, Johnny fourth from top left e 1930

THE UNKNOWN CORNER HOUSE

We now moved next door, to the house on the corner of what we really considered to be the end of Memory Lane. But it wasn't. We never knew these people, who they were, what made them tick, how many families had lived there, why they moved in, or why they moved away, yada yada yada. That is until years later, when my daughter Kaitlin befriended a girl on her high school swim team, who as it turned out, lived in this house. I would drive Kaitlin to go and visit her. Ironically, Kaitlin became our only family member to actually ever set foot in this, the unknown house on our block.

For to us, it was always 'That House,' or the house we didn't know about. The 'Question Mark' house?

That being said, we did not spend much time in front of this house. But the unknown people reminded me of an unknown part of my youth which has remained with me to this day. I always called it:

The Bat

As we would watch Yankee and Met games, Dad would tell me of a friend of his growing up who was a few years older and who was an excellent ballplayer. His name was Frank McCormick. Over a 16 year career, six of which were as an All Star, Frank played first base mainly for the Cincinnati Reds and was the National League MVP in 1940.

As kids, we had a bat that Dad told me was special; to keep it and never lose it. I have kept it and had my sons use it for their baseball games. Once it actually cracked, so we carefully nailed it and taped it together. I then used it for motivational speeches as I coached our sons' teams for years. I never knew whom it belonged to, but I am proud and thankful that it belongs now to me. Something tells me it was Frank McCormick's.

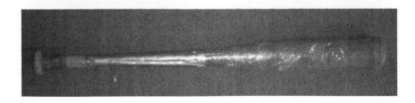

The Bat!

Our group now made our move across Maximus Road to the Eastern End of our block, a section with relatively few memories, but which deserved a charming passage through time with our family.

For it served as Mom's final chapter.

A family dinner gathering e 1978

Neighborhoods

As kids we comment about a residential area in Roslyn that had a large sign on it as we drove by on the way to Bar Beach. The placard said: 'Nob Hill.' We always wondered what life must be like inside what appeared to be a very wealthy area. We thought they had walls!

The Corner House taught me Anticipation. We then crossed the street towards Mom's final home.

THE EHOLTS

The Eholts moved onto our block and somehow made a connection with Dad. Dad was an active supporter of his very good friend, Roger Fay. During the course of this time, Randy Eholt got to know Roger and he also ventured into politics. I recalled Dad taking me along for these political movements and we once again went door to door handing out fliers promoting the Taxpayers Party Candidates. The ticket included the newcomer Randy Eholt.

Needless to say, Dad would stop and see Mr. Eholt many times over the years that they lived on our block and he was always a most welcome visitor. The four of us didn't really know what Randy Eholt did for a living as we were not close enough to his family to know. But we surely did understand that he could not support his family on a Village Trustee's stipend! Legend had it that he was also an attorney. Which would make sense, he had the handsome looks of a made for TV lawyer.

For all of our years living on Memory Lane, we believed the Taxpayer Party to always be the one in charge of our village. Many of the local officials were known to us, due to Mom and Dad's support for their friends. But we were by no means a political family, at least not at that time. Mom, however, grew heavily into it in her later years! She loved Election Night and would thrive on the excitement of being at her political headquarters sharing in the thrill of victory or the pains of defeat.

Besides the Fays, their village friends were many, including folks such as Carl Del Vecchio, then a Trustee who rose to become Mayor, and Clyde Perro, whose son went to school with Dick. Clyde was our Village Clerk. I recalled them all being very kind to us all during Dad's decline.

There was also Jack Zwiebel who was a pillar of our church and community and a very good friend of Mom and Dad's from St. Aidan's. I recalled that he and Mom had served in some of Mom's many religious groups together. Mom was very devoted to these and she was committed to their many meetings.

I believe it was at the Legion of Mary where Jack and Mom became friends. But alas, I believed that there was a mighty conflict, because Jack was a member of the opposition political party!

Jack even ran for office, fortunately not against one of Mom and Dad's friends. He became a winning member of the opposition. If my memory served correctly, eventually he also ran for Mayor but we never heard of the results.

We rolled the tape about 10 years later and I discussed making sales calls on Mr. Zwiebel while in his position for the Port Authority of NY/NJ which was then located in the beloved, historic and memorable World Trade Center. I did not and do not recall whether I ever sold him on my shipping services, but they were always most welcome visits and he always tried to teach a very green salesman everything and anything about the governmental logistics processes.

We did not discuss it during our walk, because it hadn't happened yet, but ironically, we again found my daughter Kaitlin linked to my youth through her high school friends. Years later, Kaitlin became very good friends with a classmate who was one of Jack's grandchildren. You simply can't make this up!

Most likely, thanks to Dad's membership in the Williston Park Fire Department and Mom's in the

Women's Auxiliary Group, they both made long term bonds of deep friendships. Many of which lasted far more than Dad's five years in the department. People such as the Murrays, the Howes, the Rogers, the Byrnes, the Perros, the Fays, the Del Vecchios and many others who all liked and respected the quiet A&P baker; the fellow who would coach their kids; march together proudly in the Holiday Parades; volunteer his time; and a man who had one tremendous idea based on what he did for his family; later his block; then his friends and finally for his village. Our Dad brought Santa Claus to Williston Park!

My Dad was (is?) Santa Claus!

For years, Dad would play Santa Claus for us kids. The planning for the evening was always the same and we never saw through it. We would be having our family dinner on Christmas Eve. Estelle was always there. She was a fixture in our family.

As dinner would end, we would be told that we were getting tired, and for whatever reason, we dutifully believed Estelle, Mom and Dad, and suddenly, as we were ready to go to bed, Dad always, always got some mysterious phone call requiring him to rush back to work. There was always an emergency at the bakery and a major need for Christmas pastries somewhere in the New York area. His gullible four kids fell for this *malarkey for years, and we tearfully watched our Dad sadly go off to work, missing yet another Christmas Eve. As quickly as Dad would leave, or so it seemed, suddenly Uncle Johnny would appear through our side door, always accompanied with Dad's movie camera and bright lights. It never failed, and we never saw through it!*

Estelle and Mom would wake us up from our slumber, we would march down the stairs and be overwhelmed with the joy of actually seeing Santa Claus ringing his Big Black Cow Bell shouting 'HO HO HO!'

We would sit on his lap, get a few gifts, one of which we were allowed to bring to bed with us and then Santa would gather his ever so large belly, stand up and have us all sing Christmas Carols, always ending on Jingle Bells. That must have been the cue because once that song was sung; Santa and his large white now empty bag would swiftly leave our home.

We would run to the window to try to catch a glimpse of the reindeer. While we had a fireplace, he never seemed to use it. He told us he would use it when he returned later in the evening! Fortunately for him, there rarely was a fire aglow.

Amazingly, within minutes of Santa's departure to visit our cousins' house around the corner, Dad would appear from the kitchen, come through the dining room and enter the living room, back from his mission to help the world survive yet another year with freshly made Christmas pastries! He would then join in the festivities. Year after year, we would tell Dad that he missed Santa again! And we would be assured that Santa was coming back to fill our stockings once we were all asleep in our beds.

We would then gather all around and open our gifts; one by one we would start to give our own presents to each other, specifically one by one, so the presenter and receiver could savor the moments. It was special and this was a tradition that has never ended.

If we were old enough, we would usually all go to Christmas Eve Midnight Mass, but only if we had enough tickets to this annual religious event, which would be packed with parishioners and their guests! The firemen would come in their dress uniforms and serve as honorary ushers. Everyone but Dad would come, as Dad normally had to go to work the next day - Christmas Day. For real! He really had to go to work.

When we returned from Midnight Mass, Estelle would go about the task of making us all our breakfast – around 2 A.M. It would be bacon and eggs with all of the trimmings. I really enjoyed this part of maturing – eating breakfast in the wee hours of the morning while my friends all slept!

Upon awakening, our stockings would be full. Always hung along the chimney, right where Santa could easily fill them on his return visit. However, we could not open them until Dad came home from work, normally around 3 P.M. Then we would go through it all again, another ritual of festivities with many more gifts!

We would then get together with all the kids on Memory Lane and go house to house checking out the latest gifts we all received!

Santa visits Mom and Dad's Grandchildren at our home e 1980

Santa gets a little older but still makes his visits   e 1989

As time went on, and we got to be a little older, Dad still turned into Santa Claus. He would dress up and make his visits to the children on our block. By working it out in advance with our neighbors, Dad would have them leave a bag full of presents on their front stoop in the early evening, of course only after their children went to bed. Then Dad would do his thing. Taking his large white bag along with the local phone book and big black cow bell, Dad would make a grand entrance into these homes.

As the kids gathered together, Dad would open the phone book and point out where he had these kids names listed in his master list. The kids were thrilled. He would sing with them, hug them and have pictures taken with them. He would give them the small gift that their parents had left on the stoop and tell them that he will certainly be back later with more goodies, but he needed to make another stop at their friend Johnny's house down the block and off he would go. At times he had to prove to the kids that indeed Johnny's name was in his book!

Over time, this got to be a pretty big event and the amount of Dad's house stops would increase greatly. He kept adding many people to his list, especially those friends who may have lost a loved one during the previous year. These people he would surprise and make his own visit with his own gift, to insure they knew that someone was thinking of them during the holidays. If they weren't home, he would leave his gift on their stoop, never saying whom it was from.

He carried this benevolence to other holidays – especially Easter and Mother's Day for friends who lost their husbands. The difference being he never made an announced entrance on those days. He would just get a small gift, wrap it up and mysteriously leave it on their doorstep. For years we didn't know of these ventures until a good friend of mine, who had lost his Dad, said that he finally figured out who was bringing these surprise trinkets to his home when he happened to see my Dad running away from his house and driving off in his car. I asked Dad about it and he finally opened up and told me about all the people he did this for. It was a lot of people. He said he just wanted them to know someone was thinking of them. Sadly, this could not be done in today's world, but Dad was not a creature of today, he loved and lived in a different time and it was fully appreciated by the many lives he touched.

During the course of these Santa neighborhood visits, Dad began talking to his buddies in Town Hall. He had an idea, how about we could have Santa visit all – yes ALL the children in our village. He said we could recruit many Santa's and their drivers, all sharing in the spirit of Christmas.

The Town Board voted on Dad's idea, and Operation Santa Claus was born. Some 40 years later, it is still an annual event. On Christmas Eve, around 5:30 P.M., about 45 Santa Clauses, systematically leave Williston Park Town Hall, go into their assigned drivers' cars and then head off to spread the true joy of the holidays to the many children on their lists. All thanks to Dad!

Dad's early method of having parents leave their gifts on the front stoop became enhanced. The parents started bringing the gifts to the Village Hall where they would be labeled and routed to the appropriate Santa Claus's route. Needless to say, this one village has a tremendous amount of very happy children every Christmas Eve, because they actually get to see Santa Claus enter their homes. And our Dad, a quiet, internal man, who magically would always become that jolly old man dressed in his fur trimmed red garb, had his wish come true! Dad brought Santa to our village and in a way became the real Santa Claus!

Of course the town needed drivers to maneuver Santa's sled(s). Dad's kids would sign up for that mission. I enjoyed driving Dad, I mean Santa. We would save our own neighborhood for last as it was Dad's special group. His very special group.

Over the years these last local visits became somewhat social in nature, especially when there were no children left in the house. On a cold wintry snowy night, a busy Santa would indeed get cold. Some of the neighbors would offer Santa a little sip of an adult beverage. Luckily, this was at the end of the route and everyone had a great time, Santa included.

For years on end, in the Village of Williston Park, every Christmas Holiday Season, they would hang a large picture of Santa Claus in their main lobby. Only a few of us knew who the man in the framed photo really was......here he is, a bit older, but then again, isn't Santa!

DEC. 15-1964

21 Fathers Give Santa Claus Aid

WILLISTON PARK, N.Y.

Home-to-Home Ho Ho Ho
To Bring Santa to 500

Wednesday, December 16, 1964

Baumbach Kris Kringle

While Mom and Dad may have passed away years ago, our values, memories and traditions have been maintained and strengthened. One of which is our annual Baumbach Family Kris Kringle which Mom always got much joy out of organizing. Dick, as family patriarch, does now.

With a bevy of rules to be eligible to become an official participant, (children are not included because they get their own gifts, but once you graduate college or move out of the home, you are in, and once you are engaged, your fiancé is an automatic member, etc, etc), we now have some 26 of us partake in this.

In the year 2011, one of the children endured a very serious illness and spent a considerable amount of time in the hospital away from his brother.

When it came time for the 2011 Kris Kringle, my son Kevin and his wife Jen suggested we change course for a year and perhaps pool all of the gift money and try to bring some unexpected joy to the two boys rather than spread it amongst the adults. Within seconds, the email chain was running across the country and it was a done deal. Things like this make me most proud to be a member of my family.

The Eholts taught me Ambition, and we walked some more.

THE UNKNOWN HOMES

What can one say about someone or something that no one knows anything about? This was our perplexing problem as we ended up across the street from Mom's final home where none of us had any recollection at all of who or what made these people tick. Not to mention who they were.

Three houses! Who lived, loved and took up space for oh so many years in these houses – homes? They were a mystery. Even during Mom's final time on the block, we did not recall Mom ever mentioning them.

This was quite strange, especially for Mom, for she knew all of her neighbors and took great pains to make sure they all knew her as well.

Milk Men, Mail Men, Delivery Trucks and Paper Routes

Besides our Annual Block Party, one way we got to meet the new / unknown neighbors was when the random, or what appeared to be random, delivery trucks would come rolling down the avenue. Over the course of a great stickball game, we would need to rush to the curb whenever the Krug's Bakery Truck would come and make its rounds, delivering fresh bakery products to the homes on our street. We didn't partake in that ritual. Dad made sure to take care of our daily baked goods.

As we would be lined up for a great game of Steal the Flag, down the street would come an open sided truck with all sorts of soda lined in its exposed racks. The driver would go to various homes bringing the latest sweet tooth liquid wonder. We didn't partake in that. Dad bought our sarsaparilla and root beer at the A&P or Grand Union.

"Ding Ding Ding" would mean the coming of the local knife and lawn mower blade sharpener guy. He had an incredible truck that would ring its "ding ding ding" chime and magically men and women would open their garages and come running out their doors with cutlery and blades lining up to have them sharpened with the cool whirling sound of the huge contraption on this truck. Once in a while we had our lawnmower blade sharpened; once in a while. We liked our blades dull. Hey with three boys can you blame Mom and Dad; after all I did have that 'alleged' hanging incident *lingering in my past!*

Early in the morning, some sort of milk man would venture onto our block and mysteriously place eggs and milk inside those special metallic tins that were stationed on the side steps of our neighbors homes. We didn't partake in this ritual either. Dad loved to shop; the food stores were his passion and besides, Mom found a new machine that was installed on Hillside Avenue that was always loaded with fresh milk. All you needed was a quarter and a kid to go around the corner on a bike to bring home our daily requirement of homogenized and pasteurized pleasure. We had four 'volunteers' who served that mission well!

For over twenty five years we only had two mailmen and these gentlemen proudly serviced our block. Angelo was the father of a kid in my class and he was a most beloved figure on our block. When he retired, people were upset, as he was a fixture who knew all the people on his route. Fortunately, Sandy took over. From what he had said, he was a minor league pitcher who couldn't make it to 'The Show' – meaning the Major Leagues. So he became a mail man. During my convalescence, he was a most welcome visitor when he would occasionally come into our home for a visit; oh yea, he also brought the mail! Besides, whatever anyone needed to speak about concerning the goings on our block, Sandy was the guy. He was a confidante to many and didn't tell tales out of school!

Newspapers were in our blood. Dick, Jerry and I delivered them patiently, cautiously (sure!) and sometimes reluctantly throughout both ours and the surrounding neighborhoods. Dick carried for Newsday, a tabloid – meaning its format. Dick rose to the prestigious rank of Master Carrier – I knew this was a fact since I remembered wearing his old sweatshirt which had this truth emblazoned on the front. Jerry and I delivered the Long Island Press which was in a different format, called a broadsheet....a little easier to fold except on Wednesdays and Sundays.

The only problem with the Press was that it was a seven day a week paper, while Newsday back then was only published six days. But, at least the Press brought the papers to the carrier's house to fold and deliver as opposed to Newsday where the carriers had to go and pick them up. Larry was the Long Island Press delivery guy. He was a most intriguing squatty little fellow who every Saturday morning would come to our house to get his money which we would collect starting on Thursdays.

That was the part of the job which I really hated. Asking people for money; at times begging for money. Hearing all sorts of stories as to why they didn't have it this week; 'come back again tomorrow,' or 'next week,' over and over again. Yech! My goal was to simply cover my bill each week. The good thing was that Mom and Dad became friends with Larry, who looked sort of like Louie from that classic TV show – "TAXI", and Larry and Louie seemed to share the same personality. He also repaired TV's so he got to spend a lot of time in our house! It was a lot better than Dad always buying tubes from Whelan's drugs and trying them all out!

Mom would fold the papers for Jerry and me. It was great, so when we came home from school, our papers were folded with rubber bands around them. We could then load them into our large baskets hanging over the front wheel of our bikes and off we would go.

I once needed Dad to defend me with one of my customers since I threw the paper right through their front door....crashing their glass and making a huge mess. I knocked on the door to tell them, (as if they didn't know). They were ticked. I was told to bring my father to meet them to discuss the damage, which I did. I never knew what happened after Dad talked to them, but from that moment on I was always extremely careful when I delivered their paper. Another time, I threw one paper onto a customer's roof. Not having broken anything, I didn't confess to this one. I just threw another one with a more careful aim. It was kind of weird day after day seeing this paper on their roof. Now you know why I was never a good pitcher!

Dad was a great defender of his children; he also wouldn't let anything happen to them. One day, while riding my bike back from baseball practice, I stopped at the Carvel on Hillside Avenue to take a sip of cold water from the free fountain that was on the side of the store. When I got there, I found a number of older kids there ahead of me. They wouldn't let me get any water, let alone allow me to go near the fountain. Rather they started pushing and shoving me around. Finally I managed to 'escape' and swiftly pedaled home. When I got in the house I was out of breath and scared. Dad having just arrived home from work, saw my condition, *and asked what happened. He was ticked. Into the car he took me, drove around the corner to Carvel, saw the kids, got out of the car, calmly walked over to the bunch of older boys who were still there and asked what their problem was. He then proceeded to read them the riot act about their behavior and how to best treat other kids, especially his. While I didn't go back there again for water stops, I tend to think they didn't either!*

. . . . .

Mom and Deb e 1972

The Unknowns taught me the wonder of Exploration, though I never explored their homes. We then gathered ourselves as we arrived at the end of the block and walked a few steps next door.

THE SIMMONS

When we were kids, a popular toy was a Yo-Yo. While it has enjoyed something of a renaissance in recent years, it will probably be replaced by a 'virtual' yo-yo! Basically, it is a contraption made of two small spheres of wood, split in the middle, and joined by a rounded center upon which a three foot thin string is wrapped around the core. At the end of the string, we would tie an open knot and put our ring finger through the hole. We would then be ready to fling it down to the floor, making sure however that it didn't touch the floor. With a simple snap of our wrist, magically the yo-yo would come back up to our open palm. We would spend hours doing this and no one ever heard of or suffered from carpal tunnel syndrome! (Sounds pretty lame, huh!) While I was fairly good at a trick called 'walking the dog,' Jerry was truly an expert in a trick called 'cradle the baby!' YoYo lore for yoyo aficionados!

What does this all have to do with our personal last walk on our block? Well, the house we found ourselves in front of housed the Simmons family. They had two connections to us.

Connection number one: With two girls, the Simmons were a regular All- American family, at least that's what Dick and Jerry recalled, since Deb and I didn't really know them that well. Dick was friends with their eldest daughter, Olympia who as everyone knew, went by the nickname 'Yo-Yo!' ...... Not Yo-Yo Ma!

Connection number two: As for Jerry, it was a bit different, though he would deny it vehemently, we all, and I mean all, knew that he and the Simmons' youngest daughter, Janice, were an 'item.' Geesh, in high school, or whatever time period it was, they were always together. I didn't recall Janice spending much time at our home, but I did remember Jerry spending an awful lot of his teenage years in theirs. He would up and leave and say, "I'm going to the Simmons", being very careful not to say her first name. Jerry, Deb and I didn't advertise our romances, which was far more Dick's style who really reveled in it.

Young Love

As mentioned, Dick was our family Romeo. But I was indeed the one who started young. I had a girlfriend in the first grade! Maura O'Leary was her name; she lived around the block from us. Being quite the charmer, I would carry this little redhead's books home from school while we rode the bus. I was quite the suave fellow. Her birthday was the day after mine and I would gladly go to her house and play with Maura. Our relationship ended however, when I got sick in the second grade with the measles. One afternoon Maura brought my books and homework home from school and rang the doorbell to our house. When she left, I got razzed big time by my older brothers. All I heard was: 'Ronald has a girl friend, Ronald has a girl friend, na na na na na' When I got better, I found some excuse to not carry her books home again. Peer pressure worked wonders and not only did I lose but oh so many young lassies in school did as well!

On a side note, and amusingly knowing that I will once again get whacked in the head by Jerry, I was not quite certain whether Janice was Jerry's first girl friend or was it perhaps that Hamilton girl from our vacation in Roxbury in the Catskills, NY. This was the vacation that Dick didn't go on, the one that endeared Mrs. Gates forever to Dick for advising Mom of Dick and his friends late night shenanigans at our house during his coming of age in the 1960's.

While Dick was having his own fun at home, little did he know that there was a family named Hamilton, with their bevy of young girls who were staying at the same resort that we were at. There was a gal around Jerry's age and another girl nearer to mine. I was now past first grade yet still socially scarred from the Maura O'Leary affair, leaving me truly socially stupid in matters of the fairer sex. This led to such profound thoughts and statements such as 'wow, she's pretty!' But I would leave it at that; clamming up in front of this cute little number called Kathy.

Jerry however took it to a different level and actually talked to his femme fatale Nancy. Our families spent a lot of time together at this vacation paradise, which led to additional socializing with them at their home in Brooklyn and again at ours as well.

I remembered their Dad was a bus driver for New York City, and all I could think was, 'Gees, Mr. Hamilton has the same job as Ralph Cramden!, that's so cool! 'Gee, she is pretty.' So much for my burst into teen years and why their daughter Kathy seemed to far more enjoy spending time studying for her upcoming school year rather than be with me! My mojo was missing, but alas! I would one day get it back!

Dick was our lady's man. He was born with 'mojo!' It would have been an interesting scenario had Dick come along on that vacation. First of all, he obviously wouldn't have been grounded and second of all, I think he very well may have had a 'mano a mano' contest with Jerry over Nancy, even though Nancy was a few years younger than Dick. Dick always seemed to have female companionship! Alas, the world will never know! As for the Nancy and Jerry fling – Jerry had a couple of things going against him. He lived on Long Island and Nancy lived in Brooklyn, Jerry had no car and there was no way, I mean NO WAY he would get Dad's car to go to Brooklyn for a date, hey for all we knew, he still may have been too young to drive when he dated Janice! Without wheels he was stuck in neutral.

So Jerry and Janice became an item, and we would kid him incessantly about it. Deb and I that is, for Dick it was like, what's the big deal! Jerry was coming of age and Dick was the Pro!

You know that 'WOOOOO' sound that kids do to a boy if he shows any interest in a girl? Well, Deb and I used it a lot; in fact, we both treated it as if we invented it. We would do it all the time. Saying such creative comments such as: 'Hey Jerrrrry, are you going up the block to see Janice tonight? WOOOOO!, or 'Jerrrrrry, did you see Janice today? WOOOOO!, or perhaps 'Jerry, just how is YOUR Janice doing? WOOOOO! 'etc etc.

Little did we know that WOOOOO had been around for ages. In addition, this 'Woooo' thing really did have a negative effect. For Deb her day would come. Whenever she would go out with a member of the opposite sex, she would be sure of one thing, someone in our house would say 'WOOOOO!' We would even do it to each other! I don't know about all the other loves in Jerry's life, but our family is most thankful for a blind date that Jerry had while in college. It was through that date that Jerry met his one true love, Elaine and the rest is beloved life changing history!

The Simmons taught me Tranquility.

And then we finally 'went' home.........

A

IS WHERE
THE

LIVES

HOME SWEET HOME

FINALLY OUR HOUSE

It was called a Mott Home, after the builder who constructed the block in 1929, the year of the Great Depression. One would assume it was built before October of that year, or else it would have had to have been built 10 years later under FDR's New Deal, when 1930's type stimulus packages were a national program. We never thought of our home as being old, or a product of the Depression. It was simply stated, 'home' and for a variety of reasons, it remains that way today. Home is where the heart is and this house was always home for our family! Part of us will always be there.

It's a somewhat simple three story structure, if you

include the attic, which you had to since Jerry and I slept there. It also had a full finished basement, with separate areas for a workshop; a onetime coal burner, long since converted to an oil burner heated room; a laundry room and lots of unique storage areas which included Dad's endless supply of paint, brushes, turpentine, tools, nails and screws.

The initial exterior covering was probably asbestos shingles – colored white with green trim. They were later replaced, after a series of heavy handed negotiations by Dad and some old salesman named Mr. Bock, who was selling all the neighbors some new kind of colored siding made from tar, which supposedly had built in energy efficiencies before anyone knew what energy meant! Ours would be colored green.

Our green framed windows had separately attached storm windows, which would come down in the spring and be replaced with screens. That was a task that was truly an ordeal, especially for the second floor bedrooms. Dad mastered it. He would repaint these blasted things, store them in the garage and endure a weekend of labor twice a year, washing, drying, hanging, and storing these glass shelters. As we got older, we were 'volunteered' to join in this seasonal fun.

Our garage was detached at the end of our long, at

least for us, 90 foot long driveway. The driveway was initially covered with gravel; tons and tons of tiny gray pebbles. We once tried to cover it in concrete. That is the four 'men' in the family at times tried. While I was only about eight at the time, I felt I would do my share. I remember Dick happened upon the backyard while we were busy digging. He probably came back from a date and collectively we gave him a shovel to do his share. Somebody captured this and it became a Kodak Moment!

I wish I could find that picture!

Our Time Machine

Mom and Dad decided to get a new driveway during the summer of 1959. It would be made out of a new material called blacktop. This was a major event on our block and for the 80 or so kids who lived there. It meant we would congregate and look with awe as the back hoe machine came in and dug up our old driveway, tearing it apart, picking up the chunks of dirt with its large scissor like teeth, depositing them in large containers by the street and eventually paving the driveway with new asphalt. It was a dream come true for many a ten year old, especially if it was your house where this grand event was taking place. I was so proud!

As we gazed with amazement, some of the scientific ones amongst us, and I forget who they may have been, there were so many suspects, thought that this would be a great opportunity for us to place current 'valuables' in the ground, so that some future society would be able to sell them and buy themselves a time machine to come back and visit us and take us all on a journey through time!

We then asked the construction folks when they would be digging up and covering the end of our driveway nearest the street. With a schedule firmly in hand we went to complete our tasks.

We gathered a number of specific items that we were certain would be of tremendous value a thousand years ahead in the future. We then secured a strong metal box, found some current day newspapers, food containers, including of course boxes of cereal, and whatever forms of currency we could gather, knowing it would most definitely grow in value. We deposited whatever we thought would tell future citizens what the world and life was like in the year 1959 AD. We were confident that they could then sell these treasures for an amazing fortune, and it would surely enable future folk the means to buy a high quality time machine to come back and meet us. There was a television show on TV then called Twilight Zone that featured a story on Time Travel, and all that did was confirm the theory that our resident scientists had about futuristic time travel.

We then wrote a very specific note describing who we were and left explicit instructions as to their need to purchase the best available time machine available. We didn't want some second hand machine, we wanted the very best! We said we would be waiting to meet them *at my address at 1P.M. on Wednesday, July 22nd 1959.*

We then buried the metal box of 1950's goodies. We saw it get covered with black top and as the final rolling of the asphalt occurred, we celebrated our mastery of the future with a refreshing glass of Kool Aid.

The next day at 1 P.M. we all gathered at my driveway to meet our new friends, these 'people from the future.' What would they be like? Would they be friendly? Would they try to conquer the world? Would they take us for a ride in their time machine? We surely would be famous! Obviously no one had ever thought of this plan except us!

We then talked about what our plans should be once they came. Hoping they would give us a ride, some of us wanted to go back in time and see what life was like in the 1920's, others wanted so much to see the future. No one wanted to go near the Great Depression or either of the World Wars, though the Civil War drew some interest. We were like expectant parents awaiting the birth of their firstborn!

We waited for a while, waited a bit more, then some more and thought that perhaps daylight savings time may have caused them to be confused and we agreed to wait for at least another hour. Minutes grew into hours. We waited patiently, knowing they would come. But they never did.

With parental callings for dinner, we had to cease the mission. However, we did collectively figure that this proved no one in the future ever invented a time machine. It wasn't until sometime later that one of the realists among us suggested that perhaps a new owner may have gotten a new driveway in the years to come which obviously would have destroyed our metal box. That was it! Those foolish people from the future who would someday own my house. Why couldn't they simply leave well enough alone and keep the same driveway there forever!

Did they come for us?

The children of Memory Lane had zeal and determination that was never ending. That metal memory box may still be there, buried, waiting for its futuristic discovery. That being said, if you see a bunch of people in their striped collarless shirts, dungarees and National sneakers, who appear to be in their fifties and sixties still waiting by our driveway, maybe they really know the time has now come! Some challenges are eternal and one can never stop waiting, for hope never ceases, especially on Memory Lane!

Upon coming up the three steps on our brick stoop, you would then enter our front door, which had a very detailed and unique construction. It was rounded at the top in a classic way. It was truly very nice, and for all intents and purposes it would now be considered a custom made door. It was covered by a wooden screen door which would hit you on the way in and just to be fair, also on the way out! It was truly a fanny swatter!

Our house had a very large foyer which would now be called a hallway or entrance to the home. This was so large; it had both a closet and a tall steam radiator in it as well as a side shelf for the storage of our rain boots, (back then we called them galoshes and rubbers) and those pain in the neck snow boots, which took a long while to get on but forever to take off, often being a two person job. I remember Mom trying so hard to pull them off me.

The floor of the hallway was divided in the middle and separated by a step, which became a great generational spot for Mom, Dick, Jerry and me to sit and fold our daily newspapers as we would go off delivering the news of the day to our hundreds of customers of the now defunct Long Island Press or still present Newsday. We called it the landing.

My Love Affair with The Mets

It was while sitting on the landing folding my papers when in April of 1962 I first became a true Met Fan. I recalled reading the daily stories in the Long Island Press of how in their very first year, the Mets lost their first games, every day it was the same story, another loss, they couldn't win even one game. Finally after nine losses, they finally won. In the midst of this streak, I realized this team needed a fan to stand by them, someone who could put up with their ineptness, their poor play, their buffoonery and their long look towards the future. I could wait. I was like Mom with all of her novenas to St. Jude for Hopeless Cases! I took it upon myself to be that person.

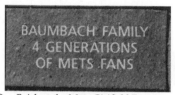

Our Brick at the Mets Citifield Entrance

My first nine games in person were all losses, but it seemed that Jerry always saw them win, so we went together. They lost!

I have been fortunate to have attended many Opening Days, one of which was in the great season of 1969 when they played the Montreal Expos in their inaugural game. The Expos played their very last game ever also against the Mets in 2004. I went to that one too!

All said, being on the Shea Stadium field to celebrate our 1969 World Series, shouting in awe in 1986 and sharing in the joy of Mets lore that started with my Mom and Dad, onto my siblings and continued with my wife, children and grandchildren has been a most delightful lifelong pleasure. Let's Go Mets!

Once you got past our foyer, there was a glass framed door which led to our very large living room. As you made your entry, your eyes would immediately be drawn to the long stairs which would take one up to the second floor and our bedrooms and then up another flight to the attic.

Our living room was a den, a family room and formal living room all in one. No one in our neighborhood had dens or family rooms back then, and if they did, we certainly didn't know who these people were!

Mom and Dad liked to be somewhat creative in their decorating. Mom took great pains to insure that she was always making what would now be a Martha Stewart look before Martha Stewart was Martha Stewart! Back then, the only available help she had to assist her was 'Hints from Heloise,' a rather cherubic, heavyset frolicking grandmother type who had a newspaper column and then a TV show based on how to get the most from your money by using everything. Everything! Frugality was the lesson of the day for those children of the Great Depression.

On the wall in front of the stairs that led to the bedrooms, which basically was on the Burke's side, (with the other wall being the Gates' side), sat our TV. The models may have changed over the years and the size may have indeed grown, but our TV remained in that spot for decades.

Perhaps they became too large for Mom to move! Whether they were black and white, color, console or simply on a TV stand, they always stayed there, and it wasn't because that was where the cable wires were; who ever heard of cable!

The first color TV we got was in the mid 50's and it was a BIG day. I remembered all of us going together to some appliance store, probably in some town called Hempstead. In fact anything we needed to buy, except for groceries seemed to come from Hempstead! I used to think that Hempstead was a store. We bought the TV, and somehow it was remarkably delivered the same day! I thought that was so cool. Same day service! Hempstead never failed us.

TV

TV's were an interesting machine then. The insides were a series of tubes and wires. If it didn't work, the standard cause of action would be to give it a whack on the top of the set. This cool trick seemed to work most times. There were also no remote controls, so kids simply became the living remotes. 'Dick, could you put on channel two, Jerry please change it to four.' Luckily there weren't too many to choose from, so we didn't get up too often. In today's age, where some folks get over 1000 channels, we managed life with a few: two-four-five-seven-nine-eleven and thirteen. Thirteen was, for us, the educational channel, a bit boring for our minds. Remember, "Sesame Street" wasn't built yet so for us, unfortunately, we were years too early to be even giving anyone directions to finding the sunny days that always shone there.

The real action was on channels two, four and seven. Five was good for cartoons, such as "Felix the Cat"; "Tweety Bird"; "Porky the Pig";"Looney Tunes" with Sandy Becker who also did "Wonderama" and Sonny Fox on "Just for Fun"; and the ever popular "The Mickey Mouse Club."

Channel nine was another kid friendly station. They would eventually, in 1962, become the first TV home of my beloved Mets. However, earlier in our lives, we would try to steer away from channel nine at 7:30 P.M. because Claude Kirschner from "Terry Tune Circus" would always close his show with the following words: 'now it's time for all little kids to go to bed!' I hated it when he said that and tried to make some distracting noise in vein hopes that Mom and Dad didn't hear him. Channel nine also had the "Million Dollar Movie"; which meant one movie would run for seven days and be on television for what seemed to be about 150 times a week. As the theme song of "Gone with the Wind" played continuously in the background, all you repeatedly heard was: 'If you missed any part of the "Million Dollar Movie"; tune in again at 9 P.M.'

The best Million Dollar Feature Movie was "King Kong." For us, it was their biggest hit. We absolutely loved it. When the big ape was shown, (okay, perhaps also "Godzilla" and "Son of Kong"); our house grew so quiet. Though I must confess, I really enjoyed viewing the "Al Jolson Story" with Dad every year. And of course, Mom couldn't get enough of "Yankee Doodle Dandy" on July 4th. As mentioned, Channel 9 also had some sports, before the Mets came along they had basketball with the Knicks, however the games were not on too often. But wrestling was! And we would gather around watching stars such as Haystacks Calhoun, Happy Humphrey and Bruno Samartino do their most amazing moves. It was so real! Nothing made up about those matches! These guys were pros!

Channel 11 had the Christmas Eve "Yule Log" and on Christmas Day they would present their annual showing of Laurel and Hardy in "The March of the Wooden Soldiers." St. Patrick's Day meant we were to watch the Parade with the Irish accent of Jack McCarthy. They also had the Yankees with Mel Allen and the 'old redhead' – Red Barber, who has a place in history for announcing the very first television broadcast of a baseball game (the Dodgers), a number of years earlier.

Our biggest thrill would be seeing Mickey Mantle hit his prodigious home runs, especially when he would come back from one of his countless spins on the disabled list due to injury. He had the uncanny ability to hit them far and high, going, going, gone! We also witnessed the incredible Maris vs. Mantle home run race in the 1961 season with both striving to hit sixty homers to break Babe Ruth's record. Maris reached sixty-one, but The Mick got hurt and ended at fifty-four. Jerry was lucky enough to be at the record breaking game!

Besides baseball, channel eleven also would show the New York Rangers on Saturday evenings and of course Jerry's favorite, Roller Derby!

But the real fun of eleven was during the afternoon as it was home to many of our classics such as Officer Joe Bolton and "The Three Stooges"; which would get Jerry and me in trouble when they had the scary episodes featuring gorillas. We would be forced to change the channel if Deb was in the room. It would be bad for her, we were told, and when it was especially stupid, we were told it was also bad for us too! Geesh, just because Moe kept poking his fingers into Larry and Curly's eyes! But the absolute best part of our Three Stooges education was the fact that Jerry could do a most incredible imitation of Curly while rolling around the floor saying: "Yuk, Yuk, Yuk!" I'll bet his grandchildren would love to see that!

Channel 11 also brought us "Bozo the Clown" right after "The Three Stooges." Come to think of it, if it was raining out, and we couldn't play outside, my day was complete!

My biggest mistake was the day that I decided to participate in the "Winky Dink" TV show. You were supposed to mail away for some special plastic sheet that would go onto your TV screen. Then you would take your magic crayons and color along with Winky. Well, I couldn't wait for the ordering process, not to mention trying to figure out how to pay for them, and I didn't really know too much about magic crayons either. What was the big deal about magic crayons? My old crayola's would work just as well! When Mom walked into the living room and saw what I did to the TV, well lets' just say, it wasn't my best day! I didn't watch too much "Winky Dink" after that! Perhaps I was then sent to a season full of both "Romper Room" and Miss Francis and her "Ding Dong School."

Oh for the days of "Felix The Cat"; "Betty Boop" (which legend had it, Mom's Mom used to babysit the real Betty Boop!; "Hopalong Cassidy"; "Roy Rogers"; "Andy's Gang"; "The Lone Ranger"; "Tales of the Texas Rangers"; Shirley Temple movies, (normally on Sunday's at 2 P.M.); "The Little Rascals" (I never tasted castor oil, but knew from my pals Spanky and Alfalfa that it tasted terrible!); "Kookla Fran and Ollie" and "The Howdy Doody Show", which Dick was oh so lucky to have been picked to sit in their Peanut Gallery! So very cool! Does the first born gets all the breaks?

"It's a bird, it's a plane, its Superman!" only meant one thing that our man of steel was about to come on and save us all from the perils of kryptonite. If he could not stop the bad guys then perhaps Bruce Wayne from "Batman"; the soldiers from "Combat"; Sergeant Joe Friday from "Dragnet"; "Highway Patrol's" Broderick Crawford or perhaps Toody and Muldoon from "Car 54 Where Are You?" could.

Mom would be watching "The Loretta Young Show," when we came home from school…she loved those large double bedroom doors. Mom's afternoon favorites also included "Queen For a Day" and "House Party" starring Art Linkletter as well "The Millionaire."

At night, the TV was the family center. Quiz shows such as "Beat The Clock" with host Bud Collyer was one of Dad's favorites, "I've Got a Secret"; "What's My Line"; which was one of Mom's; "The $64,000 Question"; all of these were staples of our viewing schedule.

"The Life of Reilly" was a hit, as were shows such as the "Arthur Godfrey Entertainment Hour"; "The Andy Williams Show"; "The Dean Martin Show"; "The Dinah Shore Show"; "The Perry Como Show"; "The Garry Moore Show", which is where we first saw Carol Burnett; "Our Miss Brooks"; "The Gale Storm Show"; "My Little Margie"; "The Bob Cummings Show'; where we all loved Schultzy who later came back to TV life as Alice in "The Brady Bunch"; "Rin Tin Tin"; "Leave it to Beaver"; "The Jack Benny Show"; "The Steve Allen Show", who was one of my personal favorite TV performers...I always loved his 'Man in the Street' bits with Louis Nye and the hilarious "Hi, ho, Steverino!"

Of course while we all loved Leo G. Carroll in "Topper"; we were scared by "Alfred Hitchcock"; learned from "You Asked For It" and were mesmerized by Rod Sterling's "Twilight Zone."

Other nighttime entertainment included "The George Burns and Gracie Allen Show"; "The Fugitive"; "Naked City"; "Dobie Gillis"; "Dr. Kildare"; "Ben Casey"; "Father Knows Best"; "Dennis The Menace"; "Lassie"; "The Bing Crosby Show"; "Name That Tune"; "The Red Skelton Hour"; "The Milton Berle

Show"; "Sergeant Preston of the Yukon"; "Ozzie and Harriet"; "My Three Sons", "Mr. Ed"; "My Favorite Martian"; "Candid Camera"; "The Jimmy Dean Show"; "The Alan Burke Show"; "The Joe Pyne Show"; "Gilligan's Island"; "The Dick Van Dyke Show"; "The Mary Tyler Moore Show"; "Rhoda"; "You Bet Your Life" with Groucho Marx'; and "Life is Worth Living" with Bishop Fulton J. Sheen, Bishop Sheen also kept us spell bound every Good Friday as we would have an annual ritual of tuning him in after coming home from church and see him reinforce the meaning of the Passion of Christ.

There would be a daily argument between Dick and I due to "American Bandstand"; because it was on the same time as my cartoons. One show no one argued about was one of my favorites: "Disneyland" which became "The Wonderful World of Disney."

"The Tonight Show" had a few early hosts such as Steve Allen, Jack Paar and Johnny Carson, with no other real competition, even though Joey Bishop and Regis Philbin once tried. Steve Allen later took on Ed Sullivan on Sunday Evenings, but couldn't topple Topo Gigio ("Eddie, kiss me goodnight!") and friends. "The Late Show" and "The Late Late Show" were really movies not talk shows and Estelle would watch them while staying up late at night on weekends at our house.

Lest we forget what happened as our channels would actually go off the air every night to rest. If we stayed up to around 2 A.M., we would see some public service *announcements, a few boring editorials, some prayers from different faith leaders, the National Anthem and then some weird 'screen savers' which would look like colored lines with a buzzing noise in the background. When the broadcast came back on again a few hours later, the National Anthem would start the programming day!*

When we walked past the TV, the wall right in front of us was where one of our 'love seats' sat. On the wall, Mom and Dad would paste wallpaper murals and over the years they would change from scenic beach views to city lights. Mom would love to decorate. Perhaps just to decorate because she never stayed with one look too long. I would kid her that during my college days her goal was to change the house every time I came home for a semester break so I wouldn't recognize it. There was always something different!

Our Living Room Wall Mural   e 1969

At the opposite side of the living room, on the Gates' side, was our fireplace, which we may have used once or twice. I always wanted to use it more often but one day some birds came in and flew all over the house. Mom freaked out and never again let us burn wood. I had argued that getting a rumbling fire going would help us prevent the birds from reentering, but the sight of those sparrows flying around her living room made a mark.

Our fireplace was reserved for Santa Claus. We also bought some fake rolling 'flame' that made all sorts of crackling sounds to help us pretend to have the glow of a real fire!

The fireplace was framed by two large chairs and both had end tables next to them. One was Mom's and one was Dad's. For years Dad sat on the chair to the left and Mom to the right and each had their own personal 'stuff' in the end table drawers. Eyeglasses, treats, paperwork, nail clippers, nail files, pens, batteries, tools, playing cards, you name it. For whatever reason, I really have no clue as to why, but suddenly in the mid 60's Mom and Dad changed sides. Dad went to right side chair and Mom to the left side chair. This broke a long tradition of household patterns. Remember Mom loved to change things around a lot! Maybe after 10 years, she needed to shake up their special seating arrangements!

Located in the front of the house was our original closed off porch, with glass framed doors separating it from the living room. In the late 50's everyone on the block wanted their house to have an 'open' look, so we joined the crowd and Dad took down the walls, studs, and doors and opened the room up masterfully.

One would never have known it was once two rooms. The break in the ceiling was hidden by some huge plastic wood looking beam that was strategically placed to appear like it was supporting the entire house. If it was, we would be in trouble! I think it was the first form of plastic ever brought into our home. It was hollow, light and strong enough to support a leaf.

Our dining room was large, very large. It held our formal dining room table, our china closet which contained Dad's mother's china which could only be used on Very Special Occasions, and a wooden server. There also were some other cabinets and odds and ends that Mom and Dad would collect to store family goodies. As kids, during family discussions, which we assumed we were not supposed to listen to, we would hide underneath the server, thinking Mom and Dad had no clue we were there. Reflecting back, there is no way they could not have realized where we were! Anyone would have seen the major clue we left 'behind' with our butts sticking out of the furniture, shaking while we tried to hold in our laughter.

The kitchen was next, and it was large, with a cool separate area called the nook, (not to be confused with a Barnes and Noble Nook!), where we had a 'U' shaped built in bench surrounding a table to sit on for dinner. Dad sat at the very front in the only chair thereby sealing off the table. You had to excuse yourself if you dare wanted to leave the dinner table early and get past Dad. It was not easy. Dad wanted the family together for dinner. Deb and I were normally stuck in the end, so no way could we get out. Dick would take the most chances and if Jerry wanted to leave he would always have some lengthy debate. However, normally Jerry stayed till the end of the meal because of one word – dessert! He had a sweet tooth that had built in GPS for the sweeter things in life!

Jerry, Ron and Deb in our living room e 1959
Dick took the picture from looking in the mirror.

Amazingly, the window on the back wall of our kitchen nook had magical skills. Whenever we closed it, any arguments that were going on inside our four walls were thought to be unheard of by any man on the outside world. I often wondered how much the Gates really heard and learned when we would have a somewhat vocal family 'Debate.' Hey every family has em', so we weren't unusual. It was probably because Dick wanted to bring another girl home for dinner!

I'll never forget one time he did indeed announce a dinner date. Mom must have really liked this girl. We all sat in the kitchen eating while Mom served Dick and his date in the dining room! Dick basically lived by the rule: 'If you don't ask, you don't get!'

Food and Things

We had our official Wednesday Ronzoni Sonna Boni Days. I think it was the law back then. They advertised it and it became second nature for everyone to have Ronzoni spaghetti. Mom would follow the law and make her most delicious version with our favorite meat sauce. Truth be told, she finally told us she also added pizza sauce to it. By the way, Estelle showed me how day old spaghetti in a frying pan made for an awesome lunch a day later.

Pizza wasn't that big a thing as 'take out' food was not that popular. We only had one local pizza parlor and it would truly have to be a special day for us to order it. More common take out was our phone call to the local Chinese restaurant for chicken chow mein. I believed it was called Gam Wah. Oh how we loved their crispy noodles in the little wax paper bag. But on the really special days, we'd have a finely grilled burger from Westons for $0.15, plus a little bag of fries! I don't recall us visiting a McDonalds or Burger King!

But perhaps the gastronomic pastimes that we enjoyed the most were a number of other dinner meals, besides Thanksgiving of course, which was a feast that Mom, or at times Dad would masterfully whip up. One meal was Mom's ground beef mixed with tomatoes and a bunch of other garden stuff. We didn't recall what this was, but we all enjoyed it. This was a staple. Then there was her stew, it was always beef! Chicken? Ah, you've got to be kidding! After all, everyone except the cows thought the more beef you ate the better for you! Another was one that we think came from Dad's sister, our Aunt Rose: tuna fish with cream of mushroom soup and noodles. To some it may not have appeared special, but it was special to us and we loved it.

Fridays was always meatless which meant fish cakes. They came from Otto's deli or the local fish store which was even better because they also had freshly made French fries. Dad and I would drive there and on the way home we would sneak them out of the oiled stained brown bag, being ever so careful to make it look like none were removed! I loved sharing that ride with Dad! The succulent aroma of the fries filled his car.

Mom and Dad would also (health nuts keep your cool), _fry_ handmade hamburgers, Dad would add eggs and bread, perhaps to stretch the meat. On summer evenings, the menu was salads. No one really barbecued back then, at least we didn't, I don't think *anyone even had a BBQ grill; we didn't for years. Instead we would have salads – tuna, potato, macaroni, cole slaw, hard boiled eggs and mayonnaise, tomatoes and mayonnaise, lettuce and mayonnaise. No one worried about butter, fat or cholesterol in mayo or nitrites in bacon. Every home had a mandatory huge jar of Crisco Fat in the cabinet. You never knew when you needed to slab a pad of that fine white stuff on the frying pan.*

We also had our 'old country' heritage food which Mom and Dad would cook with pride. Mom's own Irish soda bread, corned beef, boiled potatoes and cabbage. And of course whenever we had a ham, the next day Dad would make his pea soup, which always tasted better the second day as it got thicker. Because you also couldn't have enough pork, due to the Byrnes's connection to pork butt every month or so, an odd looking twine wrapped pork butt would find itself into our fridgerator. Some people called it a refrigerator; ours was a fridgerator or fridge.

Mom also made liver, onions and bacon (this was just for Mom and me, since no one else could stand the taste of liver). She also made a mean pork chop with sauerkraut and apple sauce. And speaking of apple sauce, it also went well with homemade potato pancakes. Come to think of it, Mom converted herself to become a true German Cook!

Saturday morning's Dad didn't work, so breakfast was pancakes. Dads were thin and Mom's were thick, which Mom often made in the summer. I never could figure out why they made them differently. And our syrup, it wasn't the Aunt Jemina brand like Ozzie and Harriet would hawk on their show, but Karo Syrup – thick and brown and oh so sweet.

On Sundays we would have breakfast after Mass because we fasted to receive Holy Communion, we would then feast on bacon (or sausage) and eggs and toast and orange juice or apple juice, or if we had intestinal issues, prune juice! On cold winter school days breakfast was an assortment of oatmeal, or perhaps "Wheatena"or "Farina." Springtime brought us cereal, not the sweetened kind, but corn flakes or some sort of huge plastic bag of wheat puffs or rice puffs which always just floated in the milk and in our stomach!

Sunday dinners were special. We would get dressed up in jackets, shirts and ties for Mass and basically stay in that garb for the day, until at least dinnertime. Dad would work six out of every seven Sundays and he would come home around 2 P.M., which meant dinner was at 2:00 P.M. not 2:30!

Sunday dinner was always, always, always in the dining room. We would use our China, not Grandma's China because Grandma's was only to be used on Thanksgiving and Christmas. I do recall Estelle methodically setting the dining room table as she would say: "knife on the right, fork on the left" or maybe it was the other way around?

Thanksgiving obviously was turkey with all the trimmings, but it always included Dad's personal Plum

Pudding and Mom's little pickled onions. Supposedly her brother John loved them. Occasionally Dad would whip up his delicious bread pudding. The staple Sunday meal was either pot roast or roast beef, with Monday's dinner being leftovers. We recalled Mom and Estelle laboring on Sundays, cutting the turnips and potatoes, mashing them, cutting celery and putting them in a special dish with olives, along with all the other fantastic foods that would fill our bountiful table.

Mom and Estelle in the kitchen preparing our Sunday Dinner e 1968

Dad came from a family of 11 and his parents lost all of their wealth during the Great Depression of 1929. He was 14 and had to drop out of school to help support his family, even though he was the third youngest. It was simply the thing to do. Dad always believed in paying bills on time, never ever going into debt, which meant not using credit cards and always having a fully stocked refrigerator and pantry. Friday afternoons meant a trip to the A&P for food shopping and we would take turns going with him. He would buy the *whole weeks groceries in one swoop and we would have a chain gang putting the food away, rolling the cans across the floor. It got a bit scary when Mom and Dad would look away and we would try to toss the egg cartons or milk containers. An event Mom and Dad didn't appreciate too much!*

You couldn't shop on Sundays as the stores were not open, in fact the only nights that stores stayed open were Thursday and Friday evenings. If you didn't get your purchasing done either during those nights or the normal workweek, or on Saturdays you simply had to wait for next week. Malls were just being born.

Our snacks were cookies, cakes and pies – our home never had a shortage of those. Oreos; those crème filled biscuits that look like wafers, animal crackers, marshmallows, mallomars, nuts, potato sticks, pretzels, and fruit. The pies were normally apple, Dutch apple, custard, pumpkin and occasionally rhubarb, which I think only Dad and Jerry ate. Anything sweet would find its way into Jerry's mouth. I don't think he ever met a cake he didn't like.

Upstairs we had our bedrooms. There were three of them. Mom and Dad had the largest, it was huge. Dick and Jerry had the next largest and Estelle had the tiny one in the front corner. It was small! But when she moved out, Dick quickly jumped at the chance for his own room. Fortunately, this got me out of Mom and Dad's bedroom and into a room to share with Jerry, which started our long history of truly being the original Odd Couple.

With Deb now in the bassinet in Mom and Dad's room, they knew something had to give. So Dad finished the attic and made a huge room out of it. Jerry and I moved upstairs, and while it didn't have heat, we would leave the attic door open to have heat come up. We never minded. The attic also didn't have air conditioning, but no one complained about the elements. No one in our neighborhood had air conditioning, perhaps no one ever heard of air conditioning! Our attic was a cool room; we even had our own shuffle board markings set up on the floor. Dad also built a bunch of what we thought were secret hideaways, actually storage sections. They were cool. We had our own special space!

Eventually Jerry couldn't take my sloppiness and actually drew a line of demarcation in the room. He had his side and I had mine. One could easily tell whose side was whose, even without his line. He never quite liked the fact that I tried to see how many days I could wear the same pair of socks before Mom would find out. I think even the socks ran downstairs by themselves to get to the washing machine! But we had fun and talked a lot at night about a lot of the things that occurred during the day, or what was planned for the next, until we fell asleep. I cherish those memories. We were sort of our own Wally and The Beav!

Dad finished our basement, and made it into a party play room. He put a bar in it and it became their special place for their New Years Eve Parties. Upon my move back home after college, I settled in there, redoing it all with Dad, including my orange and blue checkerboard carpet tiled floor, in honor of my favorite baseball team!

Our backyard wasn't large by any means, but we certainly thought it was. Our entire property lot was 40' by 100' which meant it was very narrow and our house took up most of the space. We had a small garden, a statue of the Virgin Mary, which Father Kirwin came one day to bless, and a large four person swing. Dad really enjoyed this, especially when he would take his grandchildren on long swaying swing rides as we all sadly saw his memory slowly fade away seemingly with each sway.

Desiring more outdoor living space, Dad built a patio room next to our garage, and screened it in. He was thrilled when he finished it and we would eat some of our summer meals in it. He loved it so much that he also built one with Uncle John after they both finished his basement. I am certain all of these building projects came without any instructions, or if they did, Dad would ignore them. He didn't see any real purpose in reading that stuff, he would just go about his thing and do it! And it worked!

In our backyard, we would play our own brand of baseball; we threw the ball over our house, and watch it roll down our very high roof. A bunch of us would then stand in the street waiting for the ball to hopefully come over, anxiously awaiting its expected arrival over this magnificent forty foot incline, unless it was captured by one of the dreaded gutters! Most of us simply gathered in the backyard recovering the multiple balls that couldn't quite make it over. We never broke a window, or, admitted to breaking one.

Once a year, Dad would get us in the car and off we would go to the Nassau County Police Department for their annual auction of lost or stolen property. They auctioned off cars and all sorts of stuff, but our favorite was the bicycles. Dad would take us there and we would gather our loose change and look around before the auction checking out the goods. We would then proceed to buy our newest bike! I doubt we ever spent more than a dollar and we had great bikes to ride for another year! Someone's loss became our gain!

My Uncle Eddie taking a test drive in his go cart. He looks like my son Kevin!

As kids, we would all absolutely love it when we found real treasure in someone's garbage, such as an old baby carriage. We would dissect it and take some wooden crates from the local stores, put the baby carriage wheels on them and make our own go carts, which we would race up and down the street. Un-motorized, unusual and unprofessional, but we loved them.

Next to our patio, stood our freestanding garage, which rarely, if ever, housed our car. I remembered it being filled with paint supplies, large tools, snow shovels, garden tools, ladders and Dad's treasured wooden winter windows and summer screens. What was really cool was the basketball hoop that Dad put high on its top peak. It became our very own NBA Court! We had countless games there: HORSE, One on One, Two on Two, etc. We didn't care about dunking, it wasn't allowed in the NBA then so it was not a big deal for us either. We took this very well since there was no way any of us could ever dare dunk the ball anyway!

We dribbled, passed, did layups and took outside shots, all only worth two points since there were no three point goals allowed or thought of.

On special days, Jerry and I would ride our bikes to Emery Road in Mineola and play on their fenced in court. That was the Big Time!

In our minds, we were good. In our minds, we could play with the best of them. In our minds, we appreciated what we had and in our minds and in the minds of those we grew up with, we truly had a whole lot of fun, making do with what we had, and making it better together.

Mom and Dad dancing the night away at Mom's Retirement Dinner e 1985

THE ROUND UP

We finally finished the walk on our block, our street, for basically the last time. What took many lifetimes to live took some two and a half hours to walk. Not one of us actually said, "hey this was our last walk on the block as a family," but there was no need to state the obvious. We all knew it. We have not been back there together since that day over 10 years ago. But in many ways still now, we still take the 'walk' together.

Our lives have been lovingly molded during the years we lived on this block and while we cherish it and tried to relive it, we realized it would never ever again be the same. Perhaps the experience the four of us shared, loved, craved, even at times may have hated is one that many of today's youth simply do not have the opportunity to do anymore. Our country has changed; our culture has changed; our world as we knew it has changed.

Society tells us every day that what was once a simple child's life has become a series of play dates, car pools, paid nannies, sheltered children, neighborhood watch, pre-school, after school, and so forth. The life we knew was special, but perhaps not so unique to the many other children of the fifties and sixties. But for the four of us, our block had one deep lasting memory that others surely do not have. We did it together with our

Mom and Dad, the six of us as one loving family unit on a block full of wonderful people.

Raised by the same parents, the four of us have so much in common, yet in many ways we were and are so very different. In my mind, Deb lives for the moment; Dick lives for the day; Jerry lives for the future, and as for me, well after reading this, you might say I live for the past!

If possible, I would certainly do it all over again and not change a thing. This was our family, our lives, our upbringing, our neighborhood, our history, our memories and finally, our very own shared:

Last Walk on Our Block

We did 'The Picture' one more time, a little older but still the same smiles!

Deb, Ron, Jerry and Dick

And my family taught me to Love, Honor and Obey.

The End....or is it?

The Beginning
Of the Next Chapter of Our Lives

OUR FAMILY THROUGH THE YEARS

OUR FAMILY THROUGH THE YEARS

OUR FAMILY THROUGH THE YEARS

OUR FAMILY THROUGH THE YEARS

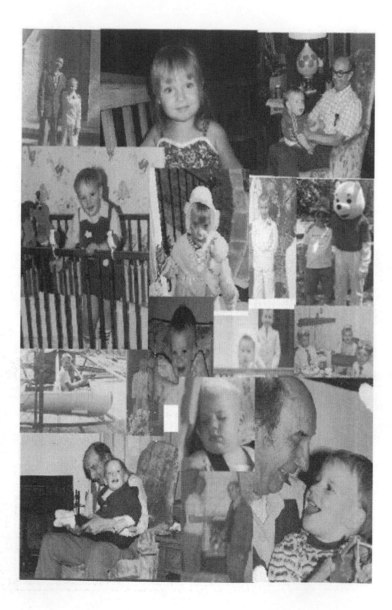

OUR FAMILY THROUGH THE YEARS

OUR FAMILY THROUGH THE YEARS

OUR FAMILY THROUGH THE YEARS

OUR FAMILY THROUGH THE YEARS

Here's To Good Friends

© *Paul Cassone 2007*

Here's to good friends, the ones we hold dear.
The ones who will tell us what we need to hear.
The ones who love us – right or wrong.
And to all those good friends I give you this song.

Life is too short - we get only one turn.
With luck we find beauty but we sometimes get burned.
But if you have a true friend or perhaps a love,
You've experienced a piece of heaven above.

Here's to good friends, the ones we hold dear.
The ones who will tell us what we need to hear.
The ones who love us – right or wrong.
And to all those good friends I give you this song.

Oh I've been so lucky and I've been so blessed.
In spite of my failings I've found success.
For I've known love and I've known good times,
And I have known friendship and written some rhymes.

Here's to good friends, the ones we hold dear.
The ones who will tell us what we need to hear.
The ones who love us – right or wrong.
And to all those good friends I give you this song.

It took me long years to write this short song.
I tried and I tried but kept getting it wrong.
I thought about my life and what had gone right,
And I realized the song was right here in plain sight.

Here's to good friends, the ones we hold dear.
The ones who will tell us what we need to hear.
The ones who love us – right or wrong.
And to all those good friends I give you this song.

Here's to good friends, the ones we hold dear.
The ones who will tell us what we need to hear.
The ones who love us – right or wrong.
And to all those good friends I give you this song.

And to all those good friends I give you this song.

With grateful appreciation to Paul Cassone for permission
http://www.myspace.com/paulcassone

A Family Remembrance

A Family Together

A Family Embrace

A Family Forever

My Grandchildren preparing for a Halloween Walk of their own!

We now invite you and yours to take your own walk on <u>your</u> block and share your memories of it on our blog on The Last Walk on Our Block website: *www.competell.com*

This Page For Your Own Walk Memories:
